THE
RETIREMENT
HANDBOOK

THE RETIREMENT HANDBOOK

An Hachette UK Company
www.hachette.co.uk

Summersdale Publishers Ltd
Part of Octopus Publishing Group Limited
Carmelite House
50 Victoria Embankment
LONDON
EC4Y 0DZ
UK

www.summersdale.com

Printed and bound in China

ISBN: 978-1-78783-698-3

THE RETIREMENT HANDBOOK

A Guide to Making the Most of Your Newfound Freedom

TED HEYBRIDGE

summersdale

Disclaimer

The author and the publisher cannot accept responsibility for any misuse or misunderstanding of any information contained herein, or any loss, damage or injury, be it health, financial or otherwise, suffered by any individual or group acting upon or relying on information contained herein. None of the views or suggestions in this book is intended to replace medical opinion from a doctor who is familiar with your particular circumstances. If you have concerns about your health, please seek professional advice.

CONTENTS

INTRODUCTION

It's a word that's been waiting for each of us all of our working lives, yet so many of us arrive at its door completely unprepared, with little idea of what to expect. Retirement is the natural conclusion of our careers and the transition into the next stage of our lives; one that can be as full of wonder, joy, discovery and purpose as any other.

If you plan for your retirement financially and socially, you will make the transition feeling in control. This is your time to spend as you choose, so it's up to you to decide how much time you wish to devote to volunteering, meeting friends, exercising, gardening or minding grandchildren. This book contains a host of advice and ideas for striking a good balance that will help you make the most of your days but still leave you with plenty of time to relax, look after your health and enjoy your hobbies.

Some people – particularly those with prestigious careers – struggle with the sudden loss of status from having an important title to being retired, so many prefer to reduce their hours gradually, continue working part-time or find a new pursuit. Learning a new skill through adult education, indulging your creative side or finding new ways to socialize are just some of the things covered here that can help you keep your mind active.

It's a challenging transition for anyone, but if managed well, you can ease yourself into retirement and continue to make a valuable contribution to the world. Be proactive and engage with the many opportunities available, maintain positive social relationships, strike up new friendships and have a whole lot of fun.

Never before have there been greater opportunities for the newly retired to enjoy a long, healthy retirement full of rewarding activities. So get reading and discover how to make the most of your newfound freedom. This next chapter of your life could be the best yet.

"RETIREMENT IS A BLANK SHEET OF PAPER. IT IS A CHANCE TO REDESIGN YOUR LIFE INTO SOMETHING NEW AND DIFFERENT."

Patrick Foley

1

STAYING ACTIVE

Physical exercise is, of course, vital all the way through our lives, but it's especially important in our latter years. We can go one of two ways as we set sail into retirement: slide into inactivity – increasing our risk of disease and shortening our life expectancy – or prioritize our fitness and remain healthy. From cycling and swimming to Zumba and yoga, this chapter looks at a few of the many sports and activities on offer to help you maintain your cardiovascular health, muscular strength and bone density. Retirement is a time for activity not complacency, and staying active promotes mental as well as physical health. Exercise releases feel-good endorphins, boosts your energy, reduces inflammation and enhances your immunity by increasing the circulation of germ-fighting immune cells and antibodies. It can also be social and fun, giving you a focus, as well as helping you stay mentally alert and aiding quality sleep. Even a small amount of daily activity such as gardening or walking will work wonders to keep you going strong for years to come.

" WE DO NOT STOP EXERCISING BECAUSE WE GROW OLD – WE GROW OLD BECAUSE WE STOP EXERCISING. "

Kenneth H. Cooper

Exercise and Your Health

The World Health Organization and national bodies share the same message: "There is strong scientific evidence that regular physical activity produces major and extensive health benefits."

Physical activity:

REDUCES RISK OF	PROMOTES
Heart disease and heart attack	Positive mental health and self-esteem
Diabetes	Heart health
High blood pressure	Healthy weight
Obesity and other weight problems	Greater energy
At least 13 different cancers	Healthy blood pressure
Depression and anxiety	Muscle tone and strength
Hip fracture and osteoporosis	Stronger bones
	Strong immune system
	Quality sleep
	Positive body image

What Are Endorphins Anyway?

When we exercise our bodies release chemicals called endorphins, which trigger a positive feeling and relieve pain. They bind to the same neuron receptors that morphine or opiates do to block pain, but unlike these drugs, this doesn't normally lead to any unhealthy addiction or dependence – although fitness fanatics may consider themselves happily addicted to exercise!

Only one in seven 65–74-year-olds and one in 14 over-75s meet World Health Organization (WHO) guidelines for recommended physical activity. These guidelines recommend 2.5 hours or more of moderate aerobic physical activity per week (for example, 30 minutes a day, five days a week – brisk walking counts. If you're already fit and active, 75 minutes per week of vigorous activity is considered equivalent). The WHO also recommends strength, balance and flexibility training two days a week.

However, any activity, no matter how light, is better than none. Light activity includes moving around your home, walking at a slow pace, cooking, vacuuming and cleaning. For older people, stretching and flexibility exercises mean you're less likely to seize up and become stiff.

Did You Know?

Research has shown that exercise is an effective treatment for mild to moderate depression and can ward off feelings of anxiety. In addition, exercise outdoors can help boost levels of vitamin D and promote positive mood.

Walking

One of the simplest and most accessible activities is walking. Everyone knows the benefits to be gained in both body and mind simply by opening the front door and stepping outside for a stroll. Extend this to include an amble through the local park, a brisk march along a windswept beach or up your nearest hill and you are well on your way to developing a passion that can deliver joy, purpose and health in equal measure. Your heart is pumping blood around your body, your breath deepens and you're getting a great workout, as well as absorbing vitamin D from the daylight. Walking can also be a social activity – you might encounter other walkers, some of whom may stop and say hello, as walkers are generally a friendly bunch. The very act of walking can put people in a positive mood.

If you crave company, consider joining a local walking group to meet new friends and discover inspiring routes. Or if you fancy combining it with travel, you could book a walking holiday to some beautiful, culturally appealing destination. If walking alone or with a dog is more your thing, many bookshops and websites offer an array of guides – regular walkers will know it's always a joy to discover new routes. For inspiration and detailed route information, invest in a walking guide or search hiking websites.

Step Away from Stress

The US National Institution for Mental Health and researchers from the University of Kansas found that regular walkers were better able to cope with stressful life changes.

Useful Apps

Downloading a plant/tree or bird identifier app can add interest and help you to identify things on your walk. Alternatively, you may prefer to leave all screens and tech at home and simply enjoy immersing yourself in the world around you.

Iconic World Walks

You could add one or two of these to your bucket list... then tick them off and add more!

Inca Trail, Peru – South America's most famous trek. A number of companies operate four-day tours, bringing walkers through ancient settlements, rocky paths and imposing mountain passes to the iconic archaeological gem of Macchu Picchu. If sheer drops, steep inclines and historic ruins aren't your thing, the Inca Trial probably isn't for you. If dramatic scenery, mountain air, friendly Peruvians and llamas are, it's hard to beat. *Moderate, camping, 45 km (28 miles).*

Chapada Diamantina, Brazil – A day-hike punctuated with high plateau views, lush vegetation and waterfalls. *Wanderlust* editor-in-chief Lyn Hughes rates this as the best one-day walk in the world. *Easy, 15 km (9 miles).*

Laugavegur, Iceland – A multi-coloured four-day hike through astonishing geological gems, with green, red, golden and purple mountains, hot springs, rivers and glaciers. *Moderate, huts, 55 km (34 miles).*

Milford Track, New Zealand – A scenic four-day hike through the South Island's alpine Fiordland from Lake Te Anau to the striking Milford Sound. Places must be pre-booked on the route, which features snow-capped alps, glacier-carved valleys, rich vegetation, dramatic falls, sparkling lakes and the 1,154-m (3,786-ft) Mackinnon Pass. *Moderate, huts, 53 km (33 miles).*

Sarangkot Pokhara, Nepal – If you fancy the three-week Annapurna Circuit but don't have the legs or willpower for something so advanced, you can't do much better than a day hike to Sarangkot Pokhara, where you'll be rewarded with panoramic views of the Himalayas. *Easy, 7 km (4 miles)*.

Great Wall of China – Sections of the 5,000-km (3,107-mile) Great Wall are not too challenging and easily accessible, especially in the Beijing area. *Easy to moderate*.

Shikoku Pilgrimage, Japan. – A 1,400-km (870-mile) trail with 1,200 years of history, but you could combine a section of this Buddhist temple-punctuated pass with a cultural trip to Japan. For a day walk, the Koyasan Choishi Michi Trail is an option. Signposts represent the Buddhist elements of earth, water, fire, air and void. For non-walkers there are cable car or bus options. *Easy, 23.5 km (14.5 miles)*.

Tsitsikamma Trail, South Africa – A six-day trek through scenic gorges and the Tsitsikamma Mountains, with wildlife, flora and views to marvel at. *Moderate, huts, 60 km (37 miles)*.

Jeju Olle, South Korea – A series of 22 relatively new trails on Jeju island, South Korea, each only 10–18 km (6–11 miles) long, totalling 347 km (215.5 miles) in all. This is an opportunity to experience a different side to South Korea, with turquoise waters, lush forest, craggy coastline, waterfalls, ocean views, dormant volcanoes and quite possibly an orange sun hanging low in the early evening sky to end your daily walk. *Easy*.

Keep the Colds Away

In addition to improving mental health, muscle tone and physical condition, exercise can improve our immune response, combat inflammation and reduce our risk of illness and disease, according to a scientific review led by David Nieman, director of Appalachian State University's Human Performance Laboratory.

Exercise increases the flow of blood and lymph through our system, which has the effect of augmenting the rate at which specialized immune cells move around our bodies, destroying viruses and bacteria. Our immune systems also generate antibodies and anti-inflammatory proteins called cytokines to help wipe out attackers. To have a lasting effect, however, the exercise needs to be regular.

Another study in the *British Journal of Sports Medicine* found that people who exercise five or more days a week had a 43 per cent lower incidence of upper respiratory tract infections (such as colds) than those who were largely inactive. Interestingly, moderate exercise is the most advantageous to immune health; overdoing it with prolonged intense exercise increases the risk of catching colds.

Cancer-combatting

A long-term study conducted by Finnish researchers concluded that those who exercised at a moderate level for at least 30 minutes a day were half as likely to develop cancer as those who were less active.

Live Longer

People who keep fit and healthy through regular exercise increase their life expectancy by over 12 years, while the highly active gain an additional five years, according to research published in the *American Journal of Epidemiology*. The message is clear: find time every day to do something physical.

Future Mirror

After the age of 25, every hour spent in front of the TV reduces your life expectancy by 22 minutes, according to research from the University of Queensland.

How do you see yourself at 90? Feeble and frail, or fighting fit, engaged and independent? Set expectations for yourself now and make them happen.

Cycling

The exhilaration of wheeling along in the outdoors and the fresh air is a joy. Cycling gets you out, relieves stress and makes you feel great. The benefits are almost as endless as the routes you could be exploring, and regular cycling significantly reduces your risk of cardiovascular disease, cancer, diabetes, depression and obesity.

Cycling is easier to fit into your daily routine than many other forms of exercise, since it doubles up as transport. If you're going to meet a friend for a coffee, why not cycle there and back if it's not too far? For those who prefer a little assistance, e-bikes can be an excellent way to get exercise but not break too much of a sweat. Biking can also be a great way to save on fuel and car maintenance, or on keeping a car in the first place.

For recreational rides, seek out scenic roads where the traffic is light, or off-road bike trails through parks or along canals. The views just get better if you tackle a national or international trail. Cycling can be a wonderfully mindful activity, and biking off-road or in the country gives you ample opportunity for observing wildlife. If cycling long distances, be sure that your bike is adjusted to fit you correctly – your local bike shop can help with this.

Well Done to the Danes

A phenomenal 63 per cent of people in Copenhagen commute to work or school by bike, making use of around 1,000 km (621 miles) of cycle lanes in the Greater Copenhagen area. According to the Cycling Embassy of Denmark, nine out of ten Danes own a bike, and 17 per cent of all journeys in Denmark are made on two wheels. Copenhagen has gone to great lengths to promote a bike-friendly culture: cycle lanes are cleared at junctions before car lanes and cyclists have their own traffic lights, complete with footrests.

The Benefits of Two Wheels

- The health benefits of cycling outweigh the injury risks by 20:1 (life years gained due to the benefits of cycling versus life years lost through injury).

- Research shows – perhaps surprisingly – that cyclists have two to three times lower exposure to pollution than car commuters, plus improved lung function.

- Since it is low impact, cycling is an excellent choice for people with osteoarthritis.

- Cycling is a benign mode of transport, reducing pollution and traffic.

- As a form of exercise, cycling can be enjoyed at any level, from low intensity to a demanding workout.

Dance, Dance, Dance

The Grey Panthers dance troupe in Darwin, Australia, say dance helps keep the mind sharp within a creative, social environment, as well as maintaining health and fitness. According to founding member Glad Morris, "It's better than taking a pill." With participants predominantly over the age of 60, they are positive role models for being active and productive members of the community, drawing on the long tradition of the respected "elder" in the culture of the indigenous people of Australia's Northern Territory.

So how about you? Is there a bit of Latin fire inside you? Perhaps the glamour of ballroom appeals? Dance is a great way to socialize and keep fit, and it can also be a way of deepening your appreciation of another culture if you explore, say, flamenco or Greek dance. To find out what's available near you, ask at your local community centre or municipal health centre, or check out dance class websites. If you're not ready to dance in public, there are plenty of DVDs or online/ YouTube classes to get you started – though remember, in a local beginner's class everyone's equally new to dancing so you're all in the same boat.

Dance Revolution

Chinese "square dancers" have been seen as troublemakers in cities across China since they began using public spaces for dancing in the mid-1990s. Using a sound system to play music, they organize themselves in lines according to ability and perform dance routines, some of which they learned as they grew up during the Cultural Revolution. It has become quite controversial, as some non-participating (often younger) local residents consider it noise pollution. However, the dancers say it is not antisocial and keeps them active, socially engaged and healthy into retirement. As many as 100 million people – mostly women in their fifties and sixties – are believed to take part.

Zumba

Developed originally in Colombia in the 1990s by an aerobics instructor who incorporated some traditional salsa and merengue into a class, Zumba has become a fitness phenomenon that anyone can enjoy. It might take a few classes to master the fancy footwork, but you'll be laughing all the way. A mix of dance and aerobics, typical routines include elements from mambo, flamenco, samba, hip-hop and tango, with a few pelvic thrusts and hip wiggles, all contributing to a fun workout that tones the muscles. There may be a class specifically for your age group.

Parkrun

Parkrun is a free, weekly community 5K open to all levels of fitness. At the time of writing, there are over 2,000 parkruns around the world across 22 countries and five continents, with four million participants. Parkrunners range from club runners to walkers keen to lose weight and get fit, with everything in between; this includes people pushing prams, parents with children, wheelchair users, blind runners with guide runners, and people running with dogs on leads. Volunteers marshal the course and offer support, and you can be home by 10 a.m. on a Saturday having run a 5K, which does wonders for your self-esteem and sense of achievement.

To register for parkrun, visit www.parkrun.com where you can select your country site and find your nearest parkrun. You don't have to be registered to take part, but you do have to register if you wish to record your time, which can aid your motivation.

Do Your Bit

If you're unsure about running or walking, register as a volunteer marshal. It's a great way to meet people, build social contacts and give your time to a great cause. Many parkrunners volunteer every so often to give something back to the community.

Social Prescribing

Parkrun UK has teamed up with the Royal College of General Practitioners to develop a national network of certified parkrun practices which prescribe parkrun and other outdoor physical activities instead of long-term medication, with great results. Parkrun has also made an impact operating in prisons.

Dr Simon Tobin, a parkrun ambassador, is a big proponent of social prescribing – "I've seen it revolutionize people's lives," he says. "As a result of coming along to parkrun, many of my patients have taken control of their health and need fewer medications. It's the best and the cheapest medicine there is."

Build It Up

- If you're new to running, start gently and build it up gradually.

- Start with 1 km, alternating between jogging and walking. Or you could jog for 60 seconds, then walk for 90 seconds and keep this going for 20 minutes. Some people find it motivating to register with a programme or app such as Couch to 5K (C25K), to help keep them on track.

- Try to run two to three times a week.

- Build it up over a few weeks until you are able to run, jog or walk a 5K. What an achievement! The hardest work is now done; the trick is to maintain this.

Yoga

Yoga is widely accepted as being beneficial for every aspect of our well-being – physical, mental, psychological and spiritual. Practising yoga regularly strengthens your core, increases muscle tone and improves flexibility, vitality, alertness, balance and breathing. It can also counteract stress and improve mood. Yoga is very adaptable, depending on your capability, and there are many types to choose from. In fact, retirement is a good time to take up yoga as you have the time to work at it, and its benefits will be valuable in later life.

Hatha is a gentle form of yoga. Find a group specifically designed for your age, or join a beginner group if you prefer a mix of ages. A good teacher will ensure you don't risk injury by moving your body incorrectly. If yoga is popular and there are plenty of practitioners in your area, you could look into Iyengar yoga, which uses props and is considered good for seniors; viniyoga, a form which adapts to the individual; or water yoga. Online classes and apps are also widely available.

Swimming

Swimming is often described as the best all-round exercise for a full-body workout. Since you're buoyant, there is little strain on the body, so it's excellent for people with limited mobility. Unless you're already an advanced swimmer, having a private lesson or two to improve your technique and breathing, and perhaps master a new stroke – butterfly, anyone? – can really pay dividends. Many swimming pools offer sessions for over-sixties if this appeals, as well as lane swimming times.

Pool-based aerobics classes such as aqua aerobics, aqua circuits, aqua Zumba and water polo are another option to try, combining the fun, structure and discipline of a class with time in the pool.

Never Too Old

Seventy-three-year-young South African Otto Thaning became the oldest man to swim the English Channel when he completed the epic 34-km (21-mile) swim from Dover to Calais in September 2014. The heart surgeon said he wanted to demonstrate what older people are capable of if they look after their health. In 2017, American Pat Gallant-Charette, then 66, became the oldest woman to swim the Channel.

Make Your Gym Membership Count

Chances are, when you were in full-time employment, you barely got time to dash to the gym and dash out again – back to work, to the supermarket, or to be home in time for dinner. Now you have the time to give your gym a proper workout! Instead of leaving straight after an exercise class or session on the machines, go for a swim or indulge in some time relaxing in the sauna, steam room or jacuzzi. Instead of sticking to the same old routines, try some of the other classes on offer, such as Pilates – excellent for core strength – or a dance/aerobics combination.

Gym Alternatives

Other activities you can join in to keep active include golf, tennis, badminton, tai chi, bowling, table tennis, jiu jitsu and even horse riding. Gardening and housekeeping are other activities that get the heart pumping.

2

HEALTH
AND
WELL-BEING

Looking after our health and well-being is about more than keeping fit – it's essential to take care of ourselves both mentally and physically as we rack up the decades. This is a time of life when we are confronted with a choice: slip into unhealthy habits, or take control of our health and well-being and reap the rewards of greater energy, improved mental agility and increased morale. This chapter looks at the importance of diet, lifestyle, psychological health and mindset. We'll explore healthy life choices, from cutting back on meat, sugar and alcohol to boosting our immune system, developing good sleep habits and staying mentally active, with a little mindfulness and meditation along the way.

" FOR MANY, RETIREMENT IS A TIME FOR PERSONAL GROWTH, WHICH BECOMES THE PATH TO GREATER PERSONAL FREEDOM. "

Robert Delamontagne

You Are What You Eat

The food we consume directly impacts on our physical and mental development. If we really want to embrace a healthy, fulfilled retirement, it's time to take a look inside ourselves, at how and what we eat and our whole mental approach to food. Essential nutrients feed every cell in our bodies and our organs rely on the vitamins and minerals we consume to sustain our life processes. These nutrients circulate around our bodies 24 hours a day as we digest and utilize the elements we need for all of our vital functions.

To ensure your body is getting what it needs, try to maintain a balance of protein, complex carbohydrates and healthy fats. The recipe is simple: eat fresh rather than processed foods, and don't overeat – one way to do this is to heed the Japanese ethos of *hara hachi bu*, which proposes eating until we are 80 per cent full.

Stay Hydrated

Drinking enough water is essential for our health; if we forget to keep our fluids up, we become dehydrated, which can lead to fatigue and poor concentration as well as thirst. The adult human body comprises an average of 57 to 60 per cent water. The average adult female needs to consume 2.2 litres (4.5 pints) of water a day; the average adult male needs 3 litres (6 pints). Water serves multiple functions in the body, including hydrating our bodies and preventing constipation, a common symptom of a Western diet. Drinking plenty of water can also make us feel fuller, making us less likely to overeat. So make sure you keep yourself hydrated throughout the day, and always have your water bottle to hand.

Water...

- is the primary building block of cells, essential to the life of every cell.
- is used by the body to metabolize and transport proteins and carbohydrates.
- is the primary component of saliva, used to digest carbohydrates and aid in swallowing.
- regulates our internal body temperature through sweating and respiration.
- insulates and acts as a shock absorber to protect the brain, spinal cord and organs.
- lubricates joints.
- flushes waste and toxins from the body in urine.

Say No to Sugar

You might recall being told that saturated fat was the root of all dietary evil, but now sugar has entered the fray as the primary culprit, charged with causing rising levels of obesity worldwide and contributing to a host of other illnesses, including heart disease, diabetes, depression, dementia, IBS, psychological problems and cancer.

Sugars take various forms, including glucose, fructose, sucrose, lactose and maltose. Fructose is converted by the liver into fat, in turn stimulating production of the fat-storage hormone insulin, which then stimulates production of the hormone leptin. If there are high levels of both hormones, the body can become resistant to them both, ultimately leading to chronic weight gain, as the body stops responding to leptin's message to curb eating to prevent further weight gain. The consumption of these sugars sends our appetite control system haywire, with the result that we feel hungry and eat more, a cycle that repeats ad infinitum. This explains why we can munch our way through a whole plate of biscuits and still want more. The fat created from consuming fructose either gets released into the bloodstream, where it increases our risk of obesity, heart disease, stroke and diabetes, or remains in the liver, where it can build up and cause fatty liver disease. Neither scenario is good.

The Solution?

Eat less sugar, and learn to see through clever marketing. Just because a product has a wholesome picture of verdant plants blowing in a breeze behind a model whose radiant complexion embodies vitality, or because it claims to be highly nutritious due to an infinitesimal amount of added minerals, doesn't mean you have to believe it. Read the labels and leave anything sugary on the shelf. Even better, make your own foods (such as granola, muesli, biscuits and sauces) and your taste buds will soon register just how sweet so many foods are.

Weighty Issue

The worldwide obesity problem has been accelerating in direct proportion to our consumption of sugar. In the US, a staggering 70.2 per cent of adults are now overweight or obese (National Institutes of Health, 2020) – 73.7 per cent of men and 66.9 per cent of women – while 67 per cent of Australian adults are overweight or obese. Mexico has the highest proportion of overweight and obese citizens at 75.2 per cent of the population. Excess sugar consumption underlies many diseases prevalent in the western world, and sugary drinks are a major contributor.

Plant Power

A diet rich in fresh, plant-based foods will do wonders for your health. Whether you choose to convert to a vegan diet for dietary, environmental and ethical reasons or continue to consume meat and fish, increasing the proportion of vegetables and fruit that you eat is the best way to boost your health naturally. Whether it's meat-free Mondays, cutting down to meat three times a week or replacing the occasional ham sandwich or chicken curry with a chickpea salad or dhal, simply increasing the amount of plant-based foods you eat is a relatively easy switch to make. Buying organic, if you can afford to, guarantees produce free from pesticide residues, together with higher welfare standards and responsible land management.

In general, raw, steamed and roasted veg (and uncooked fruit) retains more nutrients.

Super Garlic

Garlic is antiviral, antibacterial, antifungal, anti-inflammatory and immune-boosting. It has been shown to reduce the incidence and duration of colds, ease arthritis symptoms and help protect against cardiovascular disease and cancer. Other plant-based foods considered to be superfoods include leafy greens, berries, turmeric, olive oil, seaweed, tea, ginger, nuts, cocoa, chia seeds, purple corn, mushrooms and sweet potato.

Healthy, plant-based food includes every part of a plant, above and below ground. Remember to eat food from each of these plant groups a couple of times every week.

- Leaves include spinach, kale, lettuce, Brussels sprouts and cabbage.
- Stems include celery, asparagus and rhubarb.
- Seeds include sesame/chia/flax/sunflower/pumpkin seeds, sweetcorn, peas, beans and pulses.
- Fruits include aubergine, cucumber, tomato, pumpkin and berries.
- Flowers include broccoli and cauliflower.
- Roots include carrot, beetroot, parsnip, radish, turnip and swede.
- Tubers include potato, ginger, yam, turmeric, galangal, cassava and arrowroot.
- Bulbs include garlic, onions, spring onions and leeks.
- Cereals from grains include rice, wheat and corn.
- Oils from fruit/seeds/nuts include sunflower, coconut, olive and nut oils.

For over-65s, there are particular nutritional needs to consider. As we get older, we need more **protein** in order to preserve body function, muscle and lean body mass, so make sure you eat plenty of pulses and beans as well as meat (if you're a meat eater), fish and eggs.

Older adults also need to make sure they're getting enough **calcium** and **vitamin D**, to maintain good bone health. You may wish to consider a pharmaceutical grade vitamin D supplement if you don't absorb enough from daylight.

Personalized Nutrition

Recent studies suggest our diet plays a significant role in shaping the microbiome, our body's community of microbes. This in turn has a profound impact on overall health, affecting our risk of several chronic diseases, including obesity, type-2 diabetes, heart disease, IBS and cancer. The notion of "personalized nutrition" is rapidly taking hold as a scientific tool to predict individuals' metabolic responses to different foods, and prescribe dietary modifications for disease prevention.

Intermittent Fasting

Despite its recent surge in popularity, fasting dates back through human evolution and has been practised in many cultures for centuries. Hunter-gatherers didn't have access to 24-hour supermarkets and fridges full of food and often went for spells without eating. Some anthropologists believe we have evolved biologically to take advantage of these periods.

Intermittent fasting is increasingly being shown to have an impressive array of health benefits. Evidence suggests that fasting triggers protective activity on a cellular and molecular level, and supporters include bestselling health author Michael Mosley and Valter Longo. Studies suggest fasting can help reduce inflammation, blood-sugar levels, insulin resistance, arthritis and oxidative stress. It can also remove waste from cells, fight obesity, protect against and even reverse (or achieve remission from) type-2 diabetes, and improve blood pressure and resting heart rate. Since inflammation is a key driver of many common ailments, reducing inflammation reduces the risk of many diseases. Animal studies suggest intermittent fasting may also lower the risk of cancer, heart disease and cognitive decline, while promoting longevity, and results are promising in chronic pain conditions. The science also demonstrates that fasting can reset the immune system by prompting the body to produce new white blood cells and promote cellular repair.

Intermittent fasting takes various forms, but one technique is to fast for 12–16 hours as little as twice a week. This is relatively easy to achieve if you have an early dinner or skip breakfast. Older adults are advised to check with a doctor before trying any kind of fasting, and underweight people should avoid it. If you decide to try fasting, stay hydrated and eat nutrient-rich foods to keep your energy up.

Drink Less, Feel Great

You've worked all your life and you've earned this time, so why not make the most of your emancipation from the 9–5 and open a bottle every day? If this is your thinking, you'd better brace yourself, for it's important to know the many risks of alcohol and the benefits of cutting down.

Drinking alcohol affects our neurotransmitters, influencing our thoughts, feelings and actions. Alcohol is a depressant, so anxiety, depression and stress can all be amplified by drinking too much. It also increases the risk of seven cancers – mouth, upper throat, oesophageal, laryngeal, breast, bowel and liver – and can weaken the immune system.

And it doesn't stop there. Alcohol is calorific and can lead to weight gain. Carrying extra weight increases the risk of high blood pressure, which can contribute to vision loss, kidney disease and dementia. Alcohol consumption also ages skin, reduces sleep quality, damages gut health and causes inflammation, hair loss and brain shrinkage.

So consider the many benefits of drinking less instead of more, and you'll be the one with greater health, better mood, stronger immunity, a bigger brain and younger-looking skin.

Tips on Cutting Down on Alcohol

- Write down a mission statement outlining why you want to drink less and how you plan to implement this. Making a positive commitment to this decision means you're more likely to stick to it.

- Tell your friends you're choosing to cut down so they can be supportive instead of automatically topping up your glass.

- Find positive activities to replace drinking, if you use alcohol as a way to deal with stress or loneliness.

- Replace your favourite drink with a low-alcohol alternative – the same number of glasses will mean less alcohol consumed.

- Dilute alcoholic drinks, or alternate between alcoholic and non-alcoholic beverages.

- Have a glass of water before ordering your first drink – sometimes we are simply thirsty.

- Sip slowly.

- Avoid using alcohol as a reward.

- Reduce the number of days a week when you drink. On your non-drinking days, you can enjoy a non-alcoholic drink instead – try to stick to non-sugary drinks.

- Instead of meeting for a drink, suggest meeting friends for a coffee, walk or cultural night out. If you are striking up new friendships, begin on a healthy trajectory by arranging to meet for physical exercise or lunch rather than automatically suggesting going "for a drink".

Boost Your Immune System

In your latter years, your immune system may not be what it once was, but there is plenty you can do to help boost your body's defences. The immune system is a collective term for multiple systems that help fight disease, including lymph nodes, tonsils and adenoids, white blood cells, lymphocytes, bone marrow, skin, mucous membranes, the thymus and the spleen. Together, they provide defences to eliminate infections entering the body.

Harvard University researchers are exploring the effects of diet, exercise and stress on our immune response and advocate lifestyle choices to maximize our chances of staying healthy. One dietary factor affecting many older people is "micronutrient malnutrition" – **deficiency in certain essential vitamins and minerals. In this case, supplements may be recommended.**

How to ensure you have a healthy micronutrient balance:

- **Eat a varied diet high in fruit, veg, nuts and seeds.**
- **Exercise regularly.**
- **Don't smoke.**
- **Maintain a healthy weight (check your BMI).**
- **Develop a consistent sleep pattern.**
- **Have annual health checks.**
- **Get your annual flu vaccine.**
- **Minimize infections, e.g. by regular hand-washing.**
- **Keep your drinking of alcohol to a minimum.**
- **Top up vitamin D level by spending time outdoors.**

Put on a Happy Face

Smiling – even a forced, fake smile – convinces our brains to feel happier. Researchers at the University of South Australia found that the physical act of engaging the muscles we use to smile triggers a positive emotional response, even when you are simply gripping a pen between your teeth.

"When you forcefully practise smiling, it stimulates the amygdala – the emotional centre of the brain – which releases neurotransmitters to encourage an emotionally positive state," explains Dr Fernando Marmolejo-Ramos. "When your muscles say you're happy, you're more likely to see the world around you in a positive way."

The Botox Effect

In his book *The Brain: The Story of You*, neuroscientist David Eagleman expands on interesting research by psychologists David Neal and Tanya Chartrand. The research found that not only were people injected with Botox less able to mirror facial expressions that they were shown (as expected since their facial muscles are frozen), but they also struggled to identify the emotion shown. This led to the hypothesis that in order to effectively read the facial expressions of others, we rely on input and feedback from our own facial muscles.

Sweet Slumber

Quality sleep is necessary for optimal health and can affect hormone levels, mood and weight. Many people find their sleep quality reduces as they get older, and sleep apnoea is more common, so it's important to set the conditions for good sleep wherever you can. Exercise, and the other recommendations in this chapter, will help you achieve better sleep. Meanwhile, getting outside during the day and particularly in the morning can help to set your sleep cycle (circadian clock) so you are naturally tired when night falls.

During sleep, our brains cycle through four stages of sleep: three stages of non-REM (rapid eye movement) sleep essential for physical and mental well-being, and REM sleep. During the deep stage of non-REM sleep, the body repairs and grows tissue, builds bone and muscle and restores the immune system. Delta and theta brainwaves both occur during sleep; delta waves dominate when we're in a state of deep, restorative sleep.

Experts talk about "sleep hygiene", yet many of us don't give sleep the respect and priority it deserves. Sleep allows our brain and body to rest and recuperate from the day's activities, restoring our essential reserves so our bodily and mental functions can operate optimally during waking hours.

The average sleep cycle takes around 90 minutes, occurring four to six times in a good night's sleep. It isn't a circular repeating cycle but instead modulates in and out of different stages. Our deepest sleep tends to occur during the first half of the night, with longer periods of REM sleep the closer we get to waking. As we grow older, the duration of our deep sleep periods tends to decrease. If this is you, consider introducing an afternoon nap to ensure your body is getting enough restorative slow-wave sleep.

Dream a Little Dream

- Create a restful bedtime routine for yourself, perhaps with a relaxing bath, yoga sequence or book.

- Avoid caffeine and other stimulants, and make your bedroom a screen-free sanctuary.

- Give yourself the opportunity for a full 8 hours of sleep whenever you can.

- If you suffer from insomnia, sleep apnoea or another sleep problem, seek advice from a doctor or holistic health professional.

Keep Calm and Carry On

Mindfulness

Mindfulness is engaging fully with the present moment, and observing our thoughts without stopping to analyze or react to them. Many activities lend themselves naturally to mindfulness, such as gardening, DIY, arts and craft activities, cooking, performing music, participating in sports, learning a language or acquiring any new skill. Such is its effectiveness that many national and international health authorities prescribe mindfulness programmes for a range of ailments, from anxiety and depression to postnatal wellness. Why not use it as a preventative strategy rather than waiting until you might need it as a treatment?

Many people find meditation helps them to feel more grounded and balanced in their lives. Meditating helps to calm our overactive minds and can often lead to a very real sense of purpose, contentment and even enlightenment. Sometimes a brief moment of stillness and figurative quiet is all we need to achieve clarity.

Body Scan

This simple but effective meditation will help you to settle into a mindful state.

- Find a comfortable position, lying down or sitting, and focus on your breath, first observing it without judgement, then allowing it to settle, deepen and slow. You can breathe in to a count of four and out to a count of six to encourage deeper breathing, or whatever works for you.

- Perform a mental scan of your body. Starting with your toes, then the soles and tops of your feet, your ankles, calves, shins and knees, shift your focus slowly around your body. Devote a few breaths of focused attention to each body area and observe any sensations you are experiencing. Notice if you are tensing anywhere, and gently release – common areas of tension include the shoulders, jaw, tongue, forehead, forearms, buttocks, fingers and toes. Continue to breathe mindfully and release tension on an out-breath.

- If you find your mind wandering, gently let any thoughts come and go without giving them your attention.

- Allow your breathing to return to normal and continue with your day.

Brain Boot Camp

It's not only our hearts and muscles that need to work out: our brains also need exercise to stay healthy. An active brain is able to store and retrieve information more easily. So keep the grey matter fit with any kind of games and puzzles you enjoy – bridge, chess, crosswords, sudoku and cryptograms, or any kind of problem-solving exercise. Boost your brainpower by learning a new skill, language or instrument, or volunteer in an area that will broaden your horizons through interaction and benefit your cognitive functioning. Challenge yourself with a diverse range of books, audiobooks or podcasts, and you will keep your mind agile.

According to the Mayo Clinic in the US, physical activity may also help to keep memory loss at bay by increasing blood flow to the whole body – including the brain. Regular exercise improves cognitive function and reduces the risk of dementia in old age. Stimulating the mind and body, whether through volunteering, singing, a craft or dancing, will be beneficial for years to come.

3

MONEY
AND WORK

Retirement can be a joy if you can find ways to spend your time without splashing all your cash. Managing your money is vital for contentment, as financial worries inevitably cause stress. It doesn't mean you can't do anything ever again – far from it, as there are endless opportunities and discounts now available to you.

Think "streamlining" – if you're a two-car household, for example, consider how necessary that really is, and what you could do with the money you save by selling one and reducing all your maintenance, insurance and fees – not to mention the advantages of travelling under your own steam more often while your partner is using the remaining car. Give up what you don't need to own in order to have the resources to pursue what you'd really love to do. Calculate your budget and set yourself realistic financial goals, but factor in motivating indulgences to look forward to. Treats that you've earned are always more satisfying.

"THE PERIOD OF LIFE THAT MANY STILL CALL RETIREMENT, WHICH MAY EASILY INCLUDE WORKING, HAS THE POTENTIAL TO BE THE MOST TREASURED TIME IN YOUR LIFE. "

Julia Valentine

Spreadsheet Love

Use your home computer, tablet or smartphone to help with your budgeting.

- Download a budgeting template from a money planning website or see if there's already software installed on your computer. Learn to love spreadsheets and come to see them as friends that help you stay in control of your finances.

- Sit down and calculate your weekly, monthly and annual outgoings. Plot this against your income and savings, and work out how much you have left, always leaving a comfort margin – after all, none of us knows what's round the corner. You'll soon get used to balancing expenditure against income, and retaining some savings for special occasions or that proverbial rainy day. Check this regularly, perhaps on a set day of the month.

- If you need assistance with this, contact your local authority for advice or enlist the help of a financially savvy friend – you could repay your friend with advice from your area of expertise.

- Many countries operate a free money advice service for citizens – do a web search to find what's on offer in your country.

- Consider consulting a reputable financial advisor, particularly if you have multiple savings and commitments. Seeking professional advice often saves you far more than it costs.

Goodbye Tension, Hello Pension

After all those years of paying into your pension, finally it's time to do a happy dance. You're now getting reimbursed for all that work you've done over the years. The only problem is that with all that extra time now freed up, it's easy to find ways to spend your money. It's likely to be a fixed income, so work out a budget to help you see what you can afford to spend each month. Implement a routine where you budget for a few days and look forward to splashing out on something you really want on the nights that suit. You can enjoy the simple pleasures in the meantime.

Plan, Plan, Plan

- If you're not already clued up about banking and investments, get yourself on the internet and read up about all the different types on offer.

- If you haven't already done so, now is also a good time to write a will. This is particularly if you have remarried, as it can be a very contentious area.

- Plan any charitable donations or legacies you may wish to leave, consider downsizing to a more affordable and manageable home in the coming decade, and agree legal signatories or power of attorney for elderly relatives. Depending on circumstances, you may wish to seek legal advice.

Pain-Free Ways to Save

Simply by introducing some of the activities in this book, you'll be saving cash. Make shrewdness your middle name. For a start...

- Grow your own food and flowers.

- Embrace your inner chef and make your own meals. Create menu plans and buy only what you will use.

- Cycle, walk or catch the bus or train rather than driving – you are benefiting your pocket and health at the same time.

- Sell anything you don't need that's cluttering up the house.

- Find new hobbies and pursuits that are free or inexpensive – a sport, craft activity or interest in birds or wildflowers costs nothing.

- Be a savvy consumer – check a price comparison and review site when it's time to renew your utility rates, insurance premiums, phone plans, etc.

- Make sure all of your monthly outgoings are necessary.

- Make sure you're not paying to heat (or cool) rooms you don't use.

- Don't pay for TV you don't watch.

- Use a service such as Skype, Zoom, WhatsApp or Facetime for long-distance calls, so you can keep in contact with loved ones for free, and cancel phone services you don't need.

- Don't fall for marketing and hype. Do you really need the latest iWotsit?

- Review any annual subscriptions or standing orders – if you're not using these much, consider switching to pay-as-you-go.

- Make do and mend.

- Line-dry your clothes rather than using the dryer.

- Make your own cards and gifts – everyone prefers the personal touch of a home-made card.

- Turn off electrical appliances and lights when not using them.

- Use old rags for cleaning rather than buying cloths.

- Use cheap, biodegradable household products like vinegar, sodium bicarbonate and soda crystals in place of expensive cleaning products.

- Does it need to be new? Try online sites such as local Facebook, eBay, Craigslist and Freecycle.

- Can you borrow a tool you won't use very often, rather than buy it?

- Save on hotels by searching for cheaper alternatives, such as short-term rental properties.

Use Public Transport

Depending on where you live and your state pension age, you may be entitled to free bus, tram and rail travel. Plan some fun trips to see friends for a cultural city break or a recuperating couple of days in the country. You can choose to avoid busy peak travel periods, and public transport frees you up to read, listen to an audiobook or enjoy the view, instead of concentrating on the road and spending a fortune on fuel and upkeep.

You could make the most of your newfound freedom to travel for *nada* by combining your journey with other money-saving but fulfilling activities, such as a free museum and gallery tour, an historic walk, a picnic in a park or botanic garden, a sightseeing stroll, an invigorating swim or an overnight stay in a hostel. Or you could treat yourself to lunch with a friend since you've saved on travel, and perhaps a little drink, since you're not driving…

No-Spend Days

Most places in the world, including major cities, offer things to do that cost little or nothing. Whether you're staying at home or visiting somewhere new, why not look up "free things to do in…" and get some ideas?

- You're in luck if there's a local festival happening.

- Food markets can be vibrant and fun.

- Get to know the parks and waterways.

- Sit in a square in the heart of the town and people-watch. Smile!

- Many capital cities have national museums, galleries or botanic gardens with free (or donation-only) entry, while others will offer reduced admission prices for retirees, or may have a free session one evening or during a quiet part of the week.

- Discover something more about your home town by taking a route you've never explored before.

- For a different perspective, climb up the nearest big hill and take in the panoramic view, or, safety permitting, go on a night walk.

- Wild camping can be a wonderful way to embrace nature and make the most of good weather without spending a bean – provided you have a tent. Best of all, you don't have to be up early for work!

It's Off to Work We Go!

It may sound contradictory, but retirement doesn't need to mean giving up work completely. You may just want to change the way you work. If you stayed in your job most of your adult life, hopefully there will be aspects of the work you still enjoy, and now you're free to call the shots. You're the boss.

Many employers are well aware of the value of experienced staff continuing part-time into retirement. Whether you stay on the payroll or prefer to work on a freelance contract basis, you can pick the hours you work, take holidays when you like, choose the work you wish to do and still have an income – one that's small enough that it won't be heavily taxed.

If a desire to give something back and do so something socially valuable has been nagging you for years, volunteering could be more your thing, or you could launch a social enterprise or consultancy.

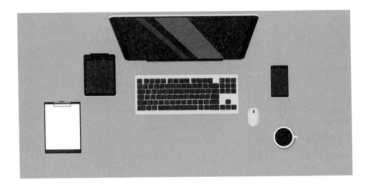

Start a Consultancy

You have banked up considerable experience during your career, and there's no reason why you can't keep on advising people and getting paid for sharing your expertise. Many of us find in middle age that our jobs are no longer fulfilling in the way they used to be; perhaps we've lost sight of the reasons we went into the job in the first place, feel undervalued or feel a lack of challenge, passion and purpose. Starting your own business can be a way of getting back to doing what you used to love, on your own terms. Working from home, you can set your own schedule, workload and objectives. Just make sure your new boss is appreciative and not too hard on you! According to a study by the London School of Economics, people who work from home are twice as content as those who work in an office.

Digital Nomad

Many people are retiring early and/or going freelance these days, either because of changes in their industry or their own disenchantment with conventional workplaces. They're developing new types of careers based on what they love. While there are other websites available to help you start a new online business, Location Rebel (www.locationrebel.com) goes a step further by allowing you to set goals and encouraging you to join a community.

Make Your Hobby Your New Job

Turning a hobby into a part-time job can give you the best of both worlds. If you love sewing baby clothes, restoring antiques, baking decadent cookies, fixing gadgets or building garden benches, and would enjoy interacting with customers either through an online site, market stall or retail outlet, your passion could bring in a little pocket money. Whatever you do, a small income from a part-time job can be the equivalent of a substantial amount of savings. And you may enjoy it so much that you never want to retire.

"Encore" Careers

What job would you have chosen if you hadn't gone into what you did? Now's your opportunity to revisit your old interests and find some new ones. If you have a particular interest, you could even deliver guest lectures or workshops at community centres, or offer to help at your local school or college.

Cornell University psychologists found that men who found another kind of work after retirement were happiest and least prone to depression. Although men are statistically more affected this way, it can of course apply to both men and women.

Give a Little Bit

Volunteering has soared in popularity in recent years, and for good reason: you're doing something amazing by giving your time, care and expertise for free, and benefiting other individuals and society at large. In sharing with others, we also benefit ourselves; we get a renewed sense of purpose and self-esteem, and we meet wonderful people. We only have one life, and many of us hit retirement and realize we want to make our time count.

The options are endless: volunteer at your local food bank, charity shop or community garden; become a befriender for an elderly person or troubled teen; provide soup and a sympathetic ear for a homeless charity; set up a local tool loan or library service; or train to be a telephone listener for a children's or emotional support charity. In relatively wealthy, peaceful cultures where many people feel privileged to have been dealt better cards than others, retirement can be the perfect time to exercise our social conscience and actively seek out something worthwhile to do with our time. For more ideas and inspiration, see Chapter 10.

4

EMBRACING NATURE

Retirement offers a fantastic opportunity to spend more time outdoors in nature, and connecting with the natural world is one of the most powerful ways of improving our quality of life.

Contemplative time in a garden, park, nature reserve or forest can restore body and soul, creating the ideal environment for our minds to settle. Once you start breathing in the fresh air, feeling that beating in your chest, observing wildlife and soaking up the views, you'll soon discover the incomparable power of connecting with nature. While adventures like hiking, kayaking or wild swimming may appeal to some, the good news is that just 2 hours a week spent in nature has proven long-term benefits to physical and mental well-being, according to a University of Exeter study. It doesn't have to be remote wilderness; any natural setting, such as parks, woods, farmland and beaches, is fine, leading to greater reported health and life satisfaction. And it makes no difference whether you catch daily chunks or indulge in a weekly nature binge – the benefits are the same.

**" IN EVERY WALK
WITH NATURE ONE
RECEIVES FAR MORE
THAN HE SEEKS. "**

John Muir

Wide-Ranging Benefits

Large-scale research by the University of East Anglia declared the health benefits of time spent outdoors to be diverse and significant. Exposure to green space, they found, reduces our risk of type-2 diabetes, cardiovascular disease, premature death and preterm birth. It also lowers heart rate, blood pressure and stress, and increases sleep duration. "One of the really interesting things we found is that exposure to green space significantly reduces people's levels of salivary cortisol – a physiological marker of stress," says the report's lead author, Caoimhe Twohig-Bennett.

Balm for the Soul

Numerous other studies have reached the same verdict: nature is good for well-being:

- The University of Michigan found that walking for 50 minutes in nature led people to perform significantly better on memory-related tasks compared to results after walking in an urban environment.

- A study in Scotland found that people who walked through a rural area "viewed their to-do list as more manageable than those who walked on city streets."

- *Medicine & Science in Sports & Exercise* reported that people walked more easily and with more positivity on an outdoor track than on an indoor treadmill.

Conservation Volunteering

Thousands of conservation charities around the world work round the clock on a huge range of environmental and conservation projects to protect species, support biodiversity and fight climate change. These range from small, local organizations to extensive national and international programmes, and many offer volunteering opportunities for various ages. Few other activities could be more rewarding, and you'll meet like-minded people as well as returning home with bucketfuls of purpose, satisfaction and perspective.

Organizations such as Frontier and Earthwatch offer international conservation volunteer trips in many exotic destinations. While the cost can be high, it's a great way to reward yourself for years of hard work and to kick off your retirement in style – perhaps paving the way for years of dedication to a whole new vocation. The Nature Conservancy, WWF and many other charities offer an array of opportunities, while Raleigh International offers volunteering management opportunities for 25–75-year-olds in many countries, including Nepal, Costa Rica and Tanzania. While some expeditions were scaled back or cancelled due to the Covid-19 pandemic, others have continued.

How you can help to do your bit:

- Tree planting
- Flood prevention and defences
- Reintroduction of native species
- Uprooting invasive non-native species of plants
- Beach plastic clean-ups
- Community education
- Species-specific conservation programmes
- Habitat regeneration
- Eco-tourism and responsible travel
- Blogging or sharing your knowledge to inspire others
- Bird/bat/owl box building
- Composting and mulching
- Dam building
- Litter picking
- Well digging and clean water system installation
- Path building
- Wetland management
- Bridge building
- Community hut building

For the Love of Wildflowers

At its most basic level, indulging a passion for wildflowers can involve nothing more than stretching one's legs. Although urban dwellers may find themselves at a disadvantage, a short bus or train ride is often all that's required to cast oneself into an unsuspected world of singular beauty and complexity. Many diverse and fascinating species of wildflowers appear in the most unpromising plots of land; all that's needed to track them down is curiosity and a keen set of eyes.

In no time at all a mild interest can develop into a full-blown passion, especially as wildflowers appear in a seasonal progression which is repeated annually, invariably in the same places. A vast range of specialist books is available to help identify individual species. And of course, there's the internet.

Not only do wildflowers provide a sensory feast and food for the soul; they are also essential for the survival of bees and other pollinators, and thus for fertilization of many plants and trees.

Planet Saviours

Wildflowers are essential for pollination, as they provide seasonal sources of nectar for insects like bees and butterflies, which in turn pollinate our food crops. They are also vital in the fight against climate change. Around the world, vast areas of wildflowers have been lost in the last 70 years to agriculture and development. In some countries, up to 97 per cent of wildflower areas have disappeared in only 45 years.

The good news is that wildflowers will grow just about anywhere. They can thrive on depleted land where hardly anything else will grow, and rewilding projects are popping up around the globe with great success. If you have outdoor space, one solution is to plant your own patch of wildflowers. Choose a mix native to your area from a seed specialist, and you will be helping to preserve your local biodiversity.

You could also encourage your local community to set aside a communal area to create a wildflower meadow, or write to your regional authority or town mayor to ask for roadside verges to be allowed to grow instead of being cut back. Many towns around the world are heeding this desire of their citizens and are allowing wildflowers to re-colonize significant roadside stretches and community sites. If there is a suitable area of wasteland near you, get campaigning!

Forest Bathing

In Japan, the practice of *shinrin-yoku*, or "forest bathing" – soaking up the atmosphere in the woods – has been a popular activity since the 1980s, after the government invested in a nationwide programme to promote health and well-being. But it's only in recent years that research into the very real therapeutic effects, led by Dr Qing Li of Nippon Medical School, Tokyo, has attracted widespread media attention.

Li, a specialist in environmental immunology, has been studying the effects of environmental chemicals, stress and lifestyle on immune function since 1988. He proposes that people should spend days at a time in the woods to get optimum health benefits, recommending it as a treatment to help prevent cancer and lifestyle-related conditions such as heart disease, diabetes, depression and hypertension.

Forest bathing was originally inspired by an ancient Buddhist practice, and the idea is to experience nature through all five senses. In order to enjoy the full benefits, leave all electronic devices at home and be present in the moment.

Tree Therapy

Forest bathing has gained recognition around the world and is enjoying a surge in popularity. Escaping to the outdoors is the natural antidote to our busy lives, and forest bathing offers the ideal activity to get us back to our roots and redress the balance. Trees are nature's air filters; via the process of photosynthesis they convert carbon dioxide into oxygen, and are helpful in reducing pollution. Even a single walk in the forest has significant benefits for respiration, and evidence suggests long-term exposure to a forest environment could reduce symptoms of respiratory illnesses such as asthma, as well as promoting better sleep. Forest bathers also experience a reduction in blood pressure and a feeling of calm.

In the western world, where we have a tendency to reach for medication when we're unwell, forest bathing offers a natural therapy for preventing and treating illness. Research suggests that phytoncides – organic compounds released by trees – have an antibacterial effect, while exposure to bacteria present in wooded areas may have inflammation-reducing benefits and boost the immune system.

Fishing

Whether or not you agree with Samuel Johnson's sentiment that "a fishing pole is a stick with a hook at one end and a fool on the other", there's no denying the attraction of fishing. This is a pastime that allows you to while away hours doing little more than sitting still in an agreeable location.

Ask a handful of anglers what motivates them and the chances are you'll receive a wealth of different replies. While catching fish is no doubt the goal of the exercise, it is not the be-all and end-all of this fascinating sport. Where some see it as simply a reason to get out of the house, others seek peace and tranquillity and the opportunity to relax in a scenic spot. There is also something meditative about fishing that allows us to forget about worldly cares or turn over ideas on anything from that night's dinner to the plot of a new novel.

A love of angling can also take you farther afield; perhaps you'll be tempted to explore a different location by planning an expedition across the country or overseas, testing your skills and introducing you to new environments and ecosystems.

Foraging

Once you know what you're looking for, foraging is truly wonderful. You're eating fresh, local plant produce in season, and the joy of finding food from nature and enjoying its nutritional and flavour benefits feels like an incredible secret. You're combining it with a walk too, so it's exercise. What can be more rewarding than going out and finding an array of beautiful, fresh, healthy food – foraged and free, a gift from nature – and then sitting down to enjoy it?

Stick to well-known plants, and avoid anything that may have been sprayed or that is too close to the road. If you wish to extend your foraging skills, buy a specialist guide, or book yourself on a foraging course with an expert.

Never pick anything you haven't identified as 100 per cent safe to eat – many plants as well as fungi and berries are highly toxic, and fatal if consumed. Once you know what you're doing, however, it's a joyful journey, and you're deepening your relationship with the land and life. Always seek permission from landowners, stick to your national countryside access regulations and only take one in 20 of what's available. Forage with respect, causing minimal damage, and you could soon be enjoying edible fruit, flowers, foliage and fungi – fresh, free and fantastic.

Embrace the Seasons

Things to Do in...

Spring

- Wander around your local woods and observe all the different buds, shoots and signs of life.

- Keep an eye out for woodland animals emerging from hibernation and watch the birds gathering moss, leaves and twigs to line their nests.

- Walk!

Summer

- Listen to the busy chatter of birds and enjoy following the progress of chicks fledging.

- Enjoy the peak of warmth, the fragrance of summer and the abundant flowering and fruiting of plants and crops.

- Walk!

Autumn

- Marvel at the range of colours that transform the landscape to a stunning palette of golds, ambers, russets and reds.

- Breathe in the autumnal smells of fungal growth and vegetation rotting down to regenerate the soil.

- Walk!

Winter

- Pause and behold the sparkling beauty of snow, frost and ice, if you're lucky enough to get these.

- Use the long nights to rest, reserve energy and get plenty of sleep in order to avoid the winter bugs and recharge your batteries for the new spring that is just around the corner.

- (You've guessed it...) Walk!

Winter Wonderland

Did winter used to be your enemy, especially during the shorter days when it was dark when you left for work and even darker when you got home? Outdoors you can rediscover the incomparable beauty of winter: a morning frost powdering the trees, crisp bright days or serene mist, together with the sense that nature is settling down to conserve energy for the spring. Committing to a long-distance walk or bike ride will awaken your senses to the pleasures of winter colours in a variety of landscapes, as long as you take care on muddy or icy tracks. You are also much likelier to enjoy peace and quiet, if that appeals, when fewer people are around.

Walkies!

As well as being a loyal companion, a dog can be a wonderful incentive to quite literally prod us to get out for a walk every day of the year, and really observe the gradual changes in the seasons.

Feathered Friends

There's nothing better to awaken an appreciation of the world we live in than watching birds. This is also one of the simplest activities a retired person can undertake, the primary requirement being the one commodity suddenly acquired: time.

Starting in your local park or garden with nothing more than your two eyes can be fulfilling enough. But, chances are, once you notice how pleasant watching birds can be, you will be inspired to purchase a guidebook and a pair of binoculars, and search further afield.

The benefits of birdwatching then begin to multiply with the introduction of fresh air and exercise. There is also the opportunity to broaden your social network, either by joining a birders' club or trusting to serendipity to connect with others while out in the field.

Every Little Helps

Why not attract garden birds to your area by buying or making a bird table or some nutritious fat-balls for winter? Specialist birdseed mixes and nuts are widely available, and it's a joyful pastime to watch all the birds that will come to visit. You could also put out a bowl of water for them to drink and wash in.

Kayaking

**❝ It's better to live one day as a lion
than 1,000 years as a lamb. ❞**

Aleksander Doba

When people talk of spending their retirement on a beach in Florida, they don't usually have in mind what Aleksander Doba did. But in April 2014, the 67-year-old adventurer from Poland arrived by kayak on New Smyrna Beach after paddling 9,656 km (6,000 miles) across the Atlantic. He had left Portugal the previous October, and completing the voyage was a dream come true – even though he had barely slept for the entire six months. He had previously paddled a kayak around the Baltic Sea and around Siberia's Lake Baikal.

You don't have to take it to such extremes, of course. Kayaking is one of the fastest-growing sports, particularly among people in their sixties and beyond, who tend to favour flat-water kayaking. Kayaks are more stable than canoes and the paddling is easier to master. Areas with plenty of protected bays or marshes are ideal. Sitting peacefully on the water, gliding gently to quiet parts of the coast inaccessible on foot, you're able to get up close to birds, fish and mammals such as seals. Sit-on-top kayaks are a good option for beginners and those who might have difficulty getting out after a long paddle.

On the Wild Side

The term "wild swimming" is often perceived as a specialist pursuit taking place in hidden wilderness spots, but anyone can enjoy wild swimming in a lake or river – in fact, that's what your ancestors probably did, before public swimming baths became widely available.

Although people have enjoyed wild swimming from time immemorial, in modern cultures many of us have lost that habit and connection. Yet this pursuit has surged in popularity, particularly since the turn of the millennium, with many people keen to reconnect with their innate wildness, indulge in a little adventure and enjoy that invigorating feeling of launching themselves into fresh (often cold) waters. One thing that wild swimming does is make you feel alive and free. Unless you're lucky enough to live near thermal waters, that initial cold can take your breath away for a second or two, before a pleasant warmth surges across your skin.

Be sure to do your research about the suitability of the water you intend to swim in before taking the plunge – more public places will have notices and more secretive spots can be found online. Swimming in water with any kind of current should always be approached with caution.

Under the Stars

Wild camping is another way to connect with the outdoors. Arrive at some idyllic spot, pitch your tent and enjoy deep discussions or singsong around a campfire, or perhaps a touch of solitude while gazing at the stars above.

If you haven't seen an old friend for a while, camping can be a magical and memorable way to rekindle that connection if they're an outdoorsy type – as long as you remember the insect repellent. Permission to erect a tent at spots not designated as campsites must be sought – and, of course, you won't necessarily have access to fresh water – though many campsites offer a more "wild" experience within their own boundaries.

Glamping

If roughing it's not your thing, many specialist accommodation providers offer a range of glamorous camping – "glamping" – options. Possibilities include stunning Mongolian yurts strung with fairy lights; fir wigwams with kitchenette and en-suite shower room; charming shepherds' huts; boutique bell tents; gypsy caravans; and luxury safari tents with Egyptian cotton bedding. Some even have their own private wood-fired hot tub!

Stargazing

> 66 **Looking up into the night sky is looking into infinity – distance is incomprehensible and therefore meaningless.** 99
>
> Douglas Adams

Whether it's the Big Dipper/Plough or the Southern Cross that dominates your night sky, stargazing can be a humbling and mind-blowing way to connect with the cosmos and no doubt entertain a profound thought or two. There's something timeless and universal about staring out into the depths of creation that is at once enlightening, humbling, magnifying and minimizing. Either you can invest in a telescope (even relatively inexpensive ones nowadays can be incredibly powerful and accurate, with various tracking settings to help you find and identify targets), or you can visit your local observatory. Let's add to Adams's quote that when we look into the night sky – at stars whose light has taken many years to reach us – we are also looking into the past.

Sail the Seven Seas

If you're fit and strong, sailing can be a wonderful skill to learn. With so many aspects to it – navigation, rigging, hoisting, knots, weather and tidal awareness, winching, steering, trimming, tacking, gybing, repairs, teamwork and leadership – it can be a surprisingly physical as well as mental activity. For people seeking challenge in retirement, sailing offers bucketfuls of demanding stimulation while also offering you ample fresh air and a connection with the elements.

Many sailing clubs offer beginner lessons to try it out, and you can work through different certifications of competence. After that, it's up to you if it's the Greek isles or a Pacific island tour. Or if flat waters are more your thing, you could try canal barges or rowing.

5

HOME AND GARDEN

There are many simple joys to be found in your own home: taking a long bath, reading, cooking and gardening, to name but a few. To make the most of your time at home, ensure that it's not a stressful place to be. Remove the clutter, and think of ways to create an even happier, healthier abode where you'll enjoy spending time alone or with friends and family.

Now is your opportunity to make your domestic space how you want it to be. You can move things around and think about design, layout and ease of use. Often, we've just stuck with the cupboard arrangement we've had for years without considering whether or not that works for us. Why not convert an old playroom into an art studio, or a cupboard into a pickling palace? If you've always dreamed of keeping chickens or bees, now you can bring those dreams to fruition.

" MAY YOUR WALLS KNOW JOY; MAY EVERY ROOM HOLD LAUGHTER AND EVERY WINDOW OPEN TO GREAT POSSIBILITY. "

Mary Anne Radmacher

Declutter Your Life

It's quite normal to hold onto things that we think might be useful, but if this gets out of hand you're in danger of developing an unhealthy hoarding habit. Here are some of the reasons why many of us have a hoarding habit:

- You make a start at clearing out your clutter and it feels like such a major undertaking that you abandon the mission. Base camp is easier than Everest. A cup of tea and a piece of cake is your escape from the task before you, but you're just delaying the inevitable...

- You've been raised to be thrifty and not throw things away.

- You don't know how long you need to keep records like tax returns.

- You've still got all the kids' clothes, plus the clothes you hope to fit into again one day.

- Emotional reasons, which can include anxiety, divorce or bereavement.

- Possessions make you feel more secure.

Acquiring "stuff" doesn't make anything better and the only way to deal with that particular stress is to tackle the clutter and get rid of what you don't need. There's no such thing as a perfect home, but if it's difficult to find things or you don't have any more space, it might be time to address the problem now to give yourself a fresh start and gain control of your home environment to make it a more relaxing place to be.

Here are some tips to start your de-cluttering:

- **Share and donate – someone needs it more than you do.**
- **Only keep what you know you will need.**
- **Only *buy* what you know you'll need – it may be beautiful, but if you're not 100 per cent sure you'll wear or use it, don't buy it.**
- **Borrow or rent rather than buy.**

Once you've de-cluttered, you should find that:

- **Fewer choices about what dish to cook or what clothes to wear lead to less stress.**
- **You'll spend less time looking for things.**
- **You'll enjoy being at home more.**

A Fresh Approach

Unless you want to sell up and move, you may be looking forward to spending a good number of years in your home, so making it a more comfortable place will reap many rewards. You'll be happier in simple pleasures and you'll feel more likely to invite people round. Painting a room can make it feel brand new, and when you put the furniture back, experiment by changing a few things, even if it's just the position of the existing furniture. Maybe you've always wanted to convert a room for a different use – perhaps as a craft room or workshop – or give your home a green makeover. Sit down and sketch out your plans, and jot down ideas about what matters to you.

Ditch Unwanted Magazines

Do you subscribe to a magazine that you never take the time to read properly? Stop the subscription and you'll feel less guilty, have less clutter and save money.

Feng Shui

To balance your space and get the right "flow", try plants and bookcases in different positions, and see how mentally calming a minimalist look can feel.

Dinner, Anyone?

With the advent of retirement, the time is ripe to branch out, expand your recipe repertoire and investigate other cuisines. How about mastering Thai curries, or producing the perfect pizza? Shelves full of beautiful cookbooks along with websites and magazines bursting with mouth-watering recipes mean there is no shortage of possibilities. TV chefs also demonstrate delicious meals in minutes, and cooking courses offer anything from the basics to specialized skills.

Make a point of seeking out local produce. Visit farmers' markets and save money – and the planet – while sourcing and purchasing the freshest and tastiest seasonal produce.

Start a Dinner Club

A dinner club can be a great way to share your home with friends, boost your social life and challenge yourself in the kitchen. Unless super-fancy is the theme, avoid one-upmanship and haute cuisine that will put off the less confident when it's their turn to host. The idea is to have a fun evening with wonderful food and company, without the costs of a restaurant. Putting some thought into music, decor, drinks, games or dinner themes can all contribute to a memorable evening that could be monthly, fortnightly or weekly.

Brew Your Own

Brewing, wine-making and cider-making all use the same process of converting sugar to alcohol, and can be an enjoyable and satisfying activity as well as providing you with a few bottles to imbibe or give away as gifts. Start off with a kit (available from brewing shops and online) and as you grow in experience, you'll be able to experiment with your own blend of ingredients and subtle differences in character.

Bread-Making

Who wants shop-bought bread with 22 ingredients when you've now got time to make your own? There are many books and web tutorials around to help you bake your own bread – anything from no-knead ciabatta to cheese and chilli loaves. You can choose from an array of flours, including ancient heritage wheat grains such as spelt and kamut and even sprouted flours, all of which are easier to digest than many modern wheat flours. Making your own bread with only a handful of ingredients – and without softeners and a dozen other additives – will do your gut health the world of good.

The Joy of Gardening

> 66 **I am once more seated under my own vine and fig tree... and hope to spend the remainder of my days in peaceful retirement, making political pursuits yield to the more rational amusement of cultivating the earth.** 99
>
> George Washington

Few pastimes can be as rewarding as keeping a garden. Whether digging, planting, pruning or simply relaxing and enjoying the fruits of your labours, a garden can do wonders for your body, mind and soul. Throughout the seasons there are different tasks to grapple with – digging, planting, pruning – and a profusion of blossoms, leaves and fruits to enjoy. Time spent in the garden gives you fresh air and exercise, and will always result in something to appreciate later, be it a beautiful place to sit, bees and butterflies attracted to your blooms, a vase of fresh flowers on the kitchen table, or a harvest of organic vegetables and herbs. If you don't have a garden, window boxes and pot plants can provide the same joy on a smaller scale.

A bird feeder is a fine addition to any garden, attracting more wildlife to help you appreciate your outdoor space. You could even design and build one yourself.

The Gardening Year

Here's a quick impression of what to expect in your garden through the seasons:

- Spring: **New bulbs poke up through the earth, buds fatten and the air is thick with a palpable sense of anticipation, energy and new life. Now is the time to prune shrubs, prepare beds, sow seeds and tidy up a little.**

- Summer: **A buzzing time of year in the garden, with plenty of jobs to keep you busy, such as weeding, watering, deadheading and mowing, plus the bonus of fresh fruit and veg and cut flowers. Make the most of the longer days and enjoy observing insects and caterpillars loving your garden as much as you do!**

- Autumn: **As leaves burst into glorious colour, the garden will need clearing and preparing for the cold winter months ahead. Essential tasks include feeding the lawn, clearing the pond and raking up fallen leaves. A great time to plant shrubs, prune fruit trees and sow winter veg.**

- Winter: **A crisp winter's day is the perfect opportunity to tidy the garden, sort out the shed, and do a spot of tool maintenance. There are still plenty of gardening tasks to get your teeth into, such as planting fruit trees and harvesting winter veg for hearty soups and stews!**

Garden Design

Get inspired to revamp your garden by visiting a show or browsing a magazine or website. Perhaps you'd like to create a peaceful corner to enjoy morning coffee and a book, brighten up a shady area, introduce more colour, create a zen space, plan for variety through the seasons, cultivate a wildflower patch or dig a pond to attract wildlife. A pebble mosaic walkway can be a beautiful feature of your outdoor space and can be achieved on a budget. Garden design can become an obsession, but a very healthy one, and your friends and neighbours will get to enjoy the fruits of your labours too.

Grow Your Own

Growing your own vegetables will cut your grocery bills, and you'll be getting the benefits of fresh organic food, clean air and exercise. If you don't have garden space, many countries and municipalities run allotment or community garden schemes. Allotments typically suit the needs of a family, and many plots include a shed. Packets of seeds cost very little and you can extend the use of your cultivating skills by learning to pickle and preserve when you have a glut. All you need is time, dedication, water (ideally rainwater) and the occasional feed (organic seaweed feed is excellent for most crops).

Some of the easiest vegetables to grow include potatoes, salad leaves, beetroot, peas, beans, courgettes, tomatoes, spinach, radishes, cucumber, chillies and basil. Not only are you reducing the food miles from farm to fork, you're also cutting down on unnecessary packaging. Best of all, you'll be picking things when they're perfectly ripe, and the less time your veggies spend in transport, the more goodness you'll gain. The sense of satisfaction when you serve up your own produce is something that can't be bought. And when it tastes delicious, you'll want to eat more. What's not to love?

Lay a Little Egg for Me

If you've got the space, now could be the time to get more ambitious in your self-sufficiency and consider a little animal husbandry.

Keeping chickens has become wildly popular in recent years and there's any number of books and websites around to get you started. As long as you can keep them safe from predators in their coop, most people find them easy to look after. They'll need food and water and mucking out – when you're away from home you'll need some help looking after them from neighbours or friends, who you can repay with the eggs they'll collect, if they eat them.

Ducks – the new chickens, some say – are an excellent alternative as they tend to stay healthier than chickens, are resilient to cold and heat, and lay rich eggs that are great for baking. They tend to be easier on the lawn, and drakes don't make the noise that roosters do. Many people keep both together, although they need slightly different feed.

Or perhaps pygmy goats or Poitou donkeys are more your thing?

Beekeeping for Beginners

Bees are garden superheroes, helping your flowers and vegetables to flourish. Many bee converts find keeping a hive an absorbing hobby, and no shelf-bought honey will ever compare to eating the honey straight from your own comb. If you end up producing more than you can use for you and your bees, you could even sell it on a market stall or from your front garden – or learn to make lip balm, candles and skin creams from the wax.

Beekeeping is an ancient art and remains a tradition practised around the world. Keepers quickly discover how fascinating and resourceful bees are, with all the different roles in the hive, from forager bees and guard bees to the queen bee herself.

One mouthful in three of the food we eat is dependent on pollination. Yet bees are threatened around the world by changes in the environment, so keeping a colony is good for everyone. Make sure you have the space and it's not prohibited in your area, and consider the initial costs of the equipment required. There's no shortage of books about beekeeping.

Spa Day at Home

❝ There must be quite a few things that a hot bath won't cure, but I don't know many of them. ❞

Sylvia Plath

There is absolutely nothing wrong with spending an hour in the bath (especially if you've just spent a few hours in the garden, or de-cluttering – it will do your muscles the world of good!). Find yourself some bath salts and a soothing essential oil, make sure there's plenty of hot water, dim the lights or light a candle, and relax. The salts will ensure you don't emerge like a prune and will feed your skin with magnesium sulphate to ease your aches. If you have trees outside your window, you could open it to hear the birdsong, or listen to an audiobook or some soft music.

After your bath, indulge yourself with a fluffy robe and some regenerating skin creams – possibly even made with your very own beeswax – and you'll feel like you've been to a luxury spa!

6

LIFELONG
LEARNING

While in full-time employment, it's understandable that opportunities for learning might seem scarce, not least because you simply don't have the time. Once retired, many people develop a longing to devote themselves to a new challenge. Now's the opportunity to continue learning a subject that was perhaps put on hold during your time in the workforce, when financial concerns took priority, or to take up something you've always longed to know more about.

If you need some structure to your day, then setting aside a few hours for learning something new will help you to appreciate the rest of your time. You can maintain a sense of purpose in your life that may otherwise feel lacking now you're not running around fulfilling business duties.

Additionally, by challenging your brain now, you're likely to stay sharp for longer, which means you can continue with a variety of interests well into old age.

" STEP OUTSIDE OF YOUR COMFORT ZONE. NEVER STOP LEARNING. NEVER STOP GROWING. "

Anonymous

Back to School

You're never too old to learn. The wisdom of this age-old maxim has never held truer than in our current world, with a seemingly endless range of institutions offering courses in a bewildering array of subjects in many different formats. Whether you want to study informally or add some letters to your name, there's almost certainly something out there for you.

Retirement offers the perfect opportunity to study that special subject which you have long been interested in but have never had the time to pursue. And the benefits of further education go beyond merely acquiring new skills. Continuing education in retirement helps people stay active and interested, promoting both physical and mental health. It also promises to bring you into contact with a broad spectrum of people, the majority of whom will be as passionate and curious about your subject as you are.

Where, what and how you study will depend upon your location and inclinations. Universities and colleges offer a selection of learning options including daytime, part-time, weekend and, increasingly, online. Evening classes cover every possible interest you can imagine (and plenty you can't), and it needn't be expensive, with concessions available for mature students.

Step It Up

Researchers believe that, as our learning levels off, the risk of dementia can increase unless we step up our intellectual activity. Anything that challenges you and expands your knowledge, such as learning a language or musical instrument or starting a new hobby, can be effective. Crosswords, sudoku… anything that keeps your mind active will help to maintain good brain health and keep you sharper for longer.

However, there's no point picking something that doesn't interest you. As a useful exercise, why not pick up a pen right now and jot down a list of possible interests and mental activities you could do to keep your mind firing on all cylinders. Car maintenance? Jewellery design? Learning Dutch?

❝ As long as you're learning, you're not old. ❞

Rosalyn S. Yalow, Winner of Nobel Prize for Medicine

U3A

Learning for learning's sake is the philosophy behind University of the Third Age (U3A). The primary goal of this international organization, which grants no qualifications and offers no assessments, is to provide education and stimulation for people in the so-called "third age" of life – the age that follows the "second age" of full-time employment and parenting and the "first age" of childhood and youth.

The U3A movement began in 1973 in France, where it is usually allied with universities. While this academic connection persists in continental Europe, the movement spread in the early 1980s, and was adapted to a cooperative-type movement run by volunteers. This model, quickly adopted by countries around the world, relies on the skills and life experiences of members, facilitated by a coordinator. Classes are sometimes led by retired university professors and other experts.

U3A group sizes vary according to demand, while between them they offer a wide choice of academic, creative and leisure activities such as art, history, music, languages, life sciences, philosophy, computing, crafts, photography and walking. It's an ideal way to explore an interest without having to sit exams. Find our more at u3a.org.uk.

Coursera

Another option ideal for extending your learning well into retirement is Coursera. Founded in 2012, Coursera is a worldwide online learning platform that offers free, accessible online courses from top universities and leading organizations. Through video lectures, quizzes and forum discussions, users can learn and gain knowledge, skills and certificates. For an additional fee, learners can enhance their qualifications with a university certificate or degree in a range of subjects including data science, business, finance, digital marketing, environment and international development. Since you undertake the courses at home in your own time, it's super-convenient, and there's the opportunity to connect with others who share the same interest.

Browse the huge list of course options at www.coursera.org.

Parlez-vous français?

There are many reasons to learn a new language. You may want to take Italian classes so you can enjoy opera more, German to read philosophers in the original language, Spanish to help you access Latin American culture and cuisine or Mandarin Chinese to broaden your cultural horizons. You may want to further understand your own roots or those of your partner, or you may simply love the sound of another language, and the idea of communicating with people from other countries and cultures.

The idea of travelling more in your hard-earned retirement years is another impetus to knuckle down to learning the language of the country you want to discover. Or, if you're hoping to retire to another country, you'll need to learn the lingo.

Language learning is something you can do at your own pace at home with books or online, but joining a class will add another social engagement to your calendar with the accompanying potential to make new friends. It will also help you keep up the momentum, and there's nothing like learning from a native speaker if your teacher is one. Alternatively, language apps like Duolingo can help you to quickly pick up useful conversational phrases, particularly if you set yourself a regular target, such as 10 minutes a day.

Carpentry

Working with your hands to build something attractive and practical can be an utterly absorbing pastime. It can also be very rewarding if you get to enjoy the fruits of your labour for years to come, or gift an item to a friend or loved one.

Carpentry is one of the oldest skills in the world, and the more you learn, the more you can make. You might be able to build anything from shelves to tables to staircases from beautiful pieces of wood, or perhaps even a wooden rocking horse for the youngest grandchild – though this would be at a fairly advanced level. It's good physical exercise and it maintains your hand–eye coordination. To learn all the skills involved, a woodworking course could prove enormously fruitful.

On a smaller scale, carving spatulas, spoons and figures can be equally satisfying.

Wine Appreciation

If you have an interest in wine, now might be the time to turn it into a passion. Offering a more varied selection of wines than the average liquor chain, independent retailers will also be able to provide expert advice on things like wine styles, regions and the matching of wine with food. Good merchants are passionate and knowledgeable about wine, and happy to pass on their knowledge. Many host in-store tastings where you can try new wines and exchange thoughts with other aficionados.

Another option is to do a course or join a group. You might even form a group of your own to swap ideas with friends and explore older and more esoteric vintages.

Wine-Tasting Tips

- Take notes. Describe colours, aromas and the wide spectrum of flavours as the wine crosses your palate. This will not only broaden your enjoyment but also increase your knowledge as you become familiar with different styles and regions.

- Augment your discoveries by reading widely. A good start is Hugh Johnson's *Pocket Wine Book*, which appears annually and is as entertaining as it is informative about regions and vintages across the globe.

Get Online

Forget "screen-agers"; it's the over-55s who have become the fastest growing demographic on social-media platforms Facebook and Twitter. Once you've retired from the workplace and are developing new roles and social networks for yourself, you may find yourself staring at a computer, tablet or phone more than you expected.

Above all, the internet is an extremely useful tool for research, information, ideas and meeting people. Platforms such as Facebook and WhatsApp are an easy way to keep up with far-flung family members, and you might also find yourself reconnecting with old friends on Zoom meetings, glass in hand, or even holding downward dog or plank positions in an online yoga class. Plus, you can do your online banking on your phone, pay bills at the press of a button and save yourself money and headaches by browsing price comparison and review sites before purchasing products and services.

Brain Training

Researchers at the Universidade do Sul de Santa Catarina in Brazil looked at data gathered from over 6,000 adults aged over 50 as part of a study on ageing, and concluded that "digital literacy", including using the internet and email, could help to delay cognitive decline and reduce memory loss.

Digital Stats

- 4.54 billion people – 60 per cent of the world population – now use the internet, according to We Are Social's Digital 2020 report (January 2020).

- 3.8 billion people around the world use social media. The report predicted that social media use would have grown to more than half the world's population by the middle of 2020.

Twitter

If you've never tried Twitter and only hear about it on the news when some celebrity disgraces themselves, you may not see the sense in it. But just like any method of communication, it can be used for positive means as well. Used wisely, it can be an excellent way of connecting with people from around the world who share similar interests, from travel to beekeeping. If you're starting a new business or hobby, you can use Twitter to build and follow a network of people who may post information and opinion relevant to you. If you've got something interesting to say from time to time, people will want to connect with you.

It's All in a Tweet

Here's how to get started:

- Choose a "handle" or username no more than 15 characters long – this may be your real name, or many users come up with something playful such as @bees_are_best if you're a beekeeper, or @potatohead if you want to share potato-growing tips!

- Write a pithy profile that will intrigue, inform or make people smile. Twitter is about saying something snappy in as few words as possible. Browse through other people's profiles to get a sense of what you think works best.

- Tweet a few tweets – messages in 280 characters or less. Let people get a sense of you through what you say. Using a hashtag to highlight the topic of your discussion will make it easier for people with similar interests to find you.

- If you wish to share another user's tweet, you can retweet or "RT" it, or quote tweet, which is retweeting and adding a comment.

- You can also pin what you consider your most relevant tweet to the top of your profile.

- Unlike some social media platforms, tweets are deletable later. However, only tweet things you're happy to have out there in the public domain as anyone could take a screenshot of your tweet.

Facebook

Social media is a rapidly and ever-changing landscape. As of 2021, Facebook still tops the social media chart in terms of general use by people of all ages, followed in second and third place by YouTube and WhatsApp. You don't have to restrict what you say to 280 characters, and most of us connect well with visuals, so many people respond to Facebook. Sure, there are continual scares about how Facebook uses what you put on there, and you should protect your privacy and other people's, but for many it's a way to keep abreast of news from friends and family.

WhatsApp

Also owned by Facebook, WhatsApp is used by many social groups to communicate messages. It's a little like texting but your message is delivered to the group on their phones, and everyone can see what everyone else writes. It's a good way to share photos and videos.

Not for You?

If social media's just not for you, that's equally fine. You won't be left behind if you keep busy with real social connections, and there's nothing to be gained in signing up to social media just because you feel you ought to.

Disinformation

There is a darker side to social media too. Much has been made of alleged interference in various state elections and referenda, including the Brazilian election of Jair Bolsonaro, where political disinformation was spread by WhatsApp to discredit the opposition. Facebook, too, has been the subject of significant controversy regarding privacy and rights.

The same rule applies across all social media: remember, you are publicly broadcasting your comments and content, so only say things you are happy to defend, post nothing offensive or defamatory, and let common sense prevail.

Podcasts

If like many people, the news is something you avoid or that evokes a lot of negative emotions, podcasts may be the antidote you're looking for. Podcasts are essentially recorded discussions that give you the joy of listening to something specific that you are interested in – topics are arranged in themes, areas of interest and popularity. They are often hosted by experts or enthusiasts in a given field, so you know you'll be getting quality content. So turn off the news notifications on your phone and tune into a podcast about one of your hobbies instead.

7

GET CREATIVE

Retirement can be a wonderful time to allow your love of the arts to flourish by visiting a wide range of museums and exhibitions, and attending concerts and author talks. It may also be your chance to unleash your creativity and express yourself more freely than ever before. Whatever your chosen medium, you'll have more time and energy to devote to it now that you're no longer pouring your soul into work. Always wanted to pursue your love of classical guitar or write a novel? Now is your chance.

"People often set interests or opportunities aside on the way out the door to pay the mortgage," says psychologist William Winn. But taking up artistic pursuits now, from picking up an instrument to throwing clay to treading the boards in amateur dramatics, may bring out something in you that you never even dreamed existed. Once again, a sense of dedication, achievement and liberation, as well as meeting new people and finding a new passion, are all potential benefits. It could even turn into a new career that might not pay as much as your last one but is more deeply rewarding.

"RETIREMENT CAN BE AN OPPORTUNITY TO ENJOY LIFE IN A NEW WAY... AND A CHANCE TO GIVE YOURSELF OVER TO NEW CHALLENGES AND ADVENTURES. "

Sara Yogev

Painting for Pleasure

"I think he's a better artist than he was a president," commented Beverly Shaver in the *Chicago Tribune* when George W. Bush's exhibition of paintings went on display at the Evanston Art Center in 2014. Bush's decision to pursue his love of painting in retirement got the thumbs-up from fellow retirees following similar artistic passions.

Painting is often a pleasure that's set aside when people are busily embroiled in the requirements of career and family life. But it's a joy to come back to in later life, partly because it's such an absorbing activity that demands focused concentration for hours at a time. Says Barbara Heaton, "It's about the process, not the product."

Signing up for an art class is an ideal way to get the creative juices flowing, but of course it doesn't have to be painting – it could be sculpture, pottery or drawing, or perhaps cartoons or photography are more your forte. If you'd rather work on your art in private at home, there are plenty of good books and websites available.

A holiday with a focus on art is also a great way to see a place in a new context.

Great Museums for Art Lovers Worldwide:

- State Hermitage Museum, St Petersburg, Russia
- Guggenheim Museum, Bilbao, Spain
- Museum of Cycladic Art, Athens, Greece
- Uffizi Gallery, Florence, Italy
- Egyptian Museum, Cairo, Egypt
- Vitra Design Museum, Weil am Rhein, Germany
- Fondation Maeght, Saint-Paul de Vence, France

- National Museum of Anthropology, Mexico City, Mexico
- Metropolitan Museum of Art, New York, USA
- Rijksmuseum, Amsterdam, Netherlands
- J. Paul Getty Museum, Los Angeles, USA
- National Museum of Modern and Contemporary Art, South Korea
- Musée d'Orsay, Paris, France
- National Gallery, London, UK

Virtual Visits

Many leading and boutique galleries around the world also offer virtual tours, classes and talks, so you can access influential art from the comfort of your kitchen. Wherever your interests lie, just do an internet search for virtual gallery tours and off you go!

Room for Reading

Retirement is traditionally a time to work through the classics of literature that you never had time for. But maybe you'd prefer to discover a whole new genre. You may feel you're well read in crime fiction or thrillers, for example, but there's a world of biography that you've barely touched upon. If you're starting a new hobby and want to learn more about it, there's a section of the library for you.

Book Groups

You can give your reading some focus by joining a book group. Perhaps there's already a local club, or maybe you and your friends could start one? Being part of a book group broadens your appreciation, spurring you to discover reads you might not otherwise have picked up. It also gives you an opportunity to discuss books and characters in depth. You'll find you think more about what you're reading and ultimately get more out of it. Publishers love reading groups, and some will offer discounts on books or extracts to download when you're choosing your next book. Another way of learning about new books, reviewing them and discussing them with others is the site www.goodreads.com.

Writing a Book

Have you always thought you've got a novel in you? Or maybe it's a memoir, or a guide on your particular field of expertise? Writing a book can take months if not years, and that's just the first draft. But if you feel the creative urge, the good news is that there's a wealth of resources to be found online to help you through the process of getting feedback on that first draft, sharing your work with a critique group or fellow writers, finding an agent and an editor and publishing the book. It's worth checking out books on the craft of writing and writers' blogs too, to improve your writing and learn about the most common telltale pitfalls that trip up many novice writers. Seek feedback from other writers – not family and friends – and learn to accept constructive criticism as a means to honing your skill.

Never Too Late...

Don't let anyone tell you it's too late to start writing. Charles Bukowski didn't publish his first novel until he was 51. Laura Ingalls Wilder didn't publish *Little House on the Prairie* until she was 64.

Publishing Your Own Book

Writing and publishing a book is deeply satisfying on many levels: the commitment involved in setting down your words, cutting and rewriting; the collaborative process of working with an editor; the interaction later with readers.

Traditional publishing is only one of the options available to writers. Particularly if you're writing a practical book that will sell to peers with similar interests, you could look into the costs and rewards of going it alone. Many authors get frustrated with the process of sending out their work to publishers and agents, only to receive rejection after rejection. By self-publishing, you retain control and can work with freelance editors and design professionals to ensure you're 100 per cent happy with the end product. These days, even established authors with traditional publishers are expected to put considerable time into promotion and marketing.

Online sites where you can share your writing and get feedback to help you improve, or self-publish online for minimal costs:

- **Authonomy**
- **Wattpad**
- **Smashwords**
- **Lulu**
- **Amazon KDP – Kindle Direct Publishing**

Beware "vanity publishers" that charge excessive fees to publish your book. Check reviews for a self-publishing platform before committing to it.

Blog It

A good way to practise your writing skills and build up an online audience is to start a blog. You get instant gratification from seeing your blog published, and feedback from your followers. You can write about pretty much anything that takes your fancy – recipes, crafts, healthy living, gardening, books and travel are all popular topics. Write in an engaging style and keep it concise – nothing will lose you readers quicker than rambling on about every detail of your day. Consult other blogs and keep your design simple, fresh and easy to navigate, with a plain, strong font – avoid a crowded, dated look.

Vlogging

Vlogging is the same as blogging, but you post video content. Again, plan what you're going to say, avoid rambling on and keep to the point. Record your video static – nothing looks more amateur than a hand-held video – and keep the background plain or relevant (if it's a gardening vlog, for example, record your video in the relevant area of your garden). Pick a single point or exercise to explain or demonstrate in each vlog – you are showing respect to your followers if you value their time.

Or, if you enjoy verbally explaining things but aren't comfortable in front of a camera, starting a podcast is another way to share your knowledge and interests with an audience.

Photography

Getting behind the lens of a camera can be a deeply rewarding hobby. Whether you prefer landscapes, nature, portraits or macro photography, exercising patience and connecting with the object you're capturing can be hugely satisfying. While some people still enjoy traditional processing, modern technology means it's incredibly easy to learn the basics of digital photography, including editing and uploading your images.

Joining a camera club could be one way to indulge your interest in photography. Regular tasks and competitions will keep you motivated and challenge your technical skills and mindset. You'll learn everything you need to know about composition, depth of field, aperture, exposure, shutter speed and lenses, and you might even find yourself leaping out of bed at 4 a.m. to capture the particular quality of the dawn light, or camping out all night to create a time-lapse of the moon.

Experiment with different styles and, if you like, start an Instagram account to share your work.

Melody Maker

Writer Diane Cole went back to playing the piano at the age of 50 after the death of her husband. She had learned piano as a child, but found her fingers too occupied with computer keyboards during the decades of work. When she needed to give her life a boost, however, her love of piano was still there.

If playing music used to give you pleasure, retirement might afford you the time to relax and enjoy practising again. Lessons to get you started can be sourced through a music shop, school, community centre or continuing education college, or via YouTube tutorials. Finding an inspiring teacher is the most important thing to augment your enjoyment and progress.

Music, Sweet Music

Researchers believe that the mental stimulation of learning a musical instrument can keep memory loss at bay. Making music can also be a very social experience, especially if you're already good enough to perform for others. Have you thought of starting up a band with some acquaintances, and writing your own music together, or even playing local gigs? If you need a bit of practice, a care home might be grateful of some live entertainment!

Join (or Start) a Choir

If you love singing, joining a choir can be a way to let loose your creative potential in a happy learning environment, with the chance to encounter people from all walks of life. Singing together has been an important part of worldwide culture throughout history and yet seldom do we get a chance to express and enjoy ourselves this way in our daily lives.

Singing in a choir has undergone something of a renaissance in the last decade. Whereas choirs often used to be seen as serious, classical, dreary or "churchy", TV choir gurus have reincarnated modern choirs as social and fun, with pop, rock, jazz and gospel music making it into the mega choirs, close harmony groups, international internet collectives and small community choirs alike.

Science has proven that singing releases endorphins that make us naturally happier, healthier and smarter. Researchers at the University of Gothenburg, Sweden, found that singing in a choir can have a calming effect that is as beneficial to health as yoga. Naturally, it's also good for the lungs, and the *Journal of Music Therapy* reported that it helps patients cope with chronic pain.

Craftmania

Crafting has become hugely popular among all age groups in recent years, so you will find an array of interesting resources on knitting, quilting, embroidery, crochet, sewing, patchwork, scrapbooking, macramé, decoupage, designing clothes or making cards. Indulge in some long-neglected pastimes, and create things that will give you pleasure. Learning a craft is in itself mentally stimulating and provides enormous satisfaction.

If you have a knack for making one-of-a-kind creations, you could join the multitude of crafters who sell what they make on craft sites Etsy or Folksy, perhaps earning a little income to pay for your supplies. Pinterest is another online site that's full of inspirational ideas.

Designing and making something personal for someone for their birthday or Christmas means so much more than buying an impersonal item from a shop. Would someone you know love a cushion covered in doggie prints or bicycles, or any design based on their favourite activity? Enjoy the process, as well as the result!

Here are a few more craft possibilities:

- **Jewellery design**
- **Pottery**
- **Woodcarving**
- **Willow/basket-weaving**

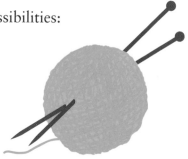

A Selection of Crafts Sold on Etsy and Folksy:

- Cushions

- Paper garlands

- Baby booties

- Lino prints

- Oak garden dibbers

- Wedding bobby pins

- Personalized fabric-covered diaries

- Brooches and earrings

- Toiletry bags

- Ceramic soap dishes

- Dog and cat beds

- Lampshades

Make Do and Mend

Restore, reuse, restyle and upcycle old clothes, upholstery, furniture, pallets and other items into new pieces. For example, if pallets come with a delivery, with a little bit of imagination and revamping you can refashion them into a coffee table or plant stand. Or a little decoupage detailing can transform a tired chest of drawers into something unique and special. For inspiration and ideas on possible upcycling projects, browse Pinterest.

Movies to Watch in Retirement

When you just need to put your feet up at the end of a long, hard day being retired, here are some top films to inspire you to even greater things the next day:

The Best Exotic Marigold Hotel – romantic comedy about a group of pensioners moving to a retirement hotel in India. Its many stars include Judi Dench and Maggie Smith.

About Schmidt – bittersweet drama about newly retired Warren Schmidt (Jack Nicholson) who begins a search for a new life and purpose after his wife dies.

Up – a Pixar animation about a curmudgeonly widower who makes a cathartic journey to Paradise Falls to honour a promise made to his wife, inadvertently bringing a young stowaway with him in his flying house. A poignant portrayal of loneliness and salvation in old age.

The Karate Kid – a touching, timeless movie centring around a cross-generational friendship, in which the good-natured teenager Daniel Larusso responds to the wisdom and life experience of his karate teacher and mentor, Mr Miyagi.

My Retirement Dreams – documentary about the American experience of growing old, following retirees in Miami struggling to leave behind their old lives and find new meaning.

Quartet – comedy drama set in a home for retired musicians. Its stars include Michael Gambon, Billy Connolly and Maggie Smith (as a bad-tempered old opera singer in need of a hip replacement).

Tatie Danielle – a marvellous black comedy that deftly subverts the benign old lady stereotype by playing on preconceptions about the elderly. The 82-year-old heroine Danielle is no sweet old dear; she's manipulative and mean, and this French film cleverly suggests that old people are a mix of good and bad, just like everyone else.

Calendar Girls – if you're thinking of raising money for charity, this comedy about a group of Women's Institute ladies in Yorkshire, England, might give you some ideas…

Amateur Dramatics

Many communities have an amateur theatre group that puts on performances. If you enjoy drama, this might be a chance to get involved. Start off by volunteering behind the scenes with costumes, sets or selling tickets if you like contact with people (and you'll likely be rewarded for your efforts in being allowed into shows for free). Alternatively, seek out a senior theatre group where you'll make new friends and where there might be more scope for acting opportunities. If you have a background in performing or have always wanted to audition for a role, ask around to see what the procedure is within the group.

Making a Song and Dance about Retirement

A cabaret of song and dance performed by a theatrical group in Darwin, Australia, called *Reluctant Retirees*, traced the journey of two women about to retire. One looked forward to the happy work-free days; the other feared a loss of identity once she lost the connection with her workplace. In the end, both found there was never enough time to do everything that retirement offered.

8

RELATIONSHIPS

Here's a piece of good news: simply spending time with friends and relatives is good for you. Talking on the phone or getting together for a chat helps keep you sharp and can lower your blood pressure. Socializing has been proven to be just as effective as crosswords at boosting your intellectual prowess. So, a new hobby that involves meeting people can do you the world of good.

Retirement is not only a good opportunity to consolidate friendships – you can spend more time doing things with your partner and develop a close bond with the grandkids. You could have some surprises in store. Retirement may allow a more sociable and compassionate you to develop. If you don't currently have a partner and are feeling lonely, the opportunities for meeting someone with similar interests are about to begin.

"THOSE WHO LOVE DEEP NEVER GROW OLD. "

Arthur Wing Pinero

De-Stress with Friends

Retirement can be a wonderful time for spending more time with good pals. Socializing with friends is one of the simplest and most effective things we can all do to combat stress – not to mention have fun – and social networks are widely acknowledged as effective aids for our mental health and for combatting anxiety and depression. In *The Depression Cure*, Dr Steve Ilardi lists social connectedness as one of six steps to beat depression without drugs.

Researchers at the London School of Economics found that people's moods improved the most when they were with friends. It's not the number of friends you have that counts; it's the quality and depth of those friendships. A small number of close friends whom you can trust, talk to about anything and rely on for support is far more meaningful than an army of social contacts who aren't real friends. Going into older age, however, any social connections are beneficial and help prevent social isolation.

Now that you're removed from your network of colleagues, supportive friendships will become a lifesaver. It's essential to be able to share your emotions with others as you adjust to the major life change of retirement. Companions can help you cope – and you can listen to, help and support them too.

Love and Marriage

Who knew your other half had such annoying habits? Just as well you don't have any...

You've most likely never spent so much time together. It's a joy, but it's also terrifying when you think about it, isn't it? Assuming at least one of you worked outside the home, you're probably used to spending about 6 hours a day in one another's company. If you double that in retirement, there's bound to be tension from time to time. Do you have common goals for retirement? If not, will you support one another's dreams either by joining the other or spending some time apart?

Make sure you have separate interests and see your own friends. That way, you'll have something to talk about when you get home. On the other hand, this may be a great opportunity to do a renovation project or start a business together, and see your partnership develop in an exciting new way. Be gentle with your partner if one of you retires first – chances are it's not as easy as it looks for the other half.

Just the Two of Us

After money, the most common worry about retirement is how it will affect your marriage. Even in the healthiest of relationships, suddenly being thrown together for so much time can be a major strain.

One of the most common concerns is about invasion of personal space. You can prepare in advance for this eventuality by encouraging your partner to pursue a new interest in retirement, and by doing the same yourself. Healthy time apart really is the secret to mutually appreciated time together. It doesn't matter if your time apart is with friends or pursuing a new activity, as long as it's stimulating and fulfilling. Then you'll be in a better mood for all those hours together at home.

Be patient and give your partner space and time to adjust. Whether it's both or just one of you who's retired, it is an adjustment for you both.

The secrets to a successful relationship after retirement:

- **Maintain your own interests – and perhaps introduce some shared ones.**

- **Divide and share household chores fairly.**

- **Treat each other with kindness – if you have developed a default habit of griping at each other, notice this, and try to speak to your partner the way you would speak to a friend.**

- Communicate when you're not happy about some aspect of your relationship.

66 **The problems come when one or both partners has the 'oh-god-nothing-to-do' syndrome... Find something interesting, or steer your other half toward an interest if they are out of practice at finding one for themselves. And talk to one another.** 99

66 **My husband drove me mad when he first retired – until I got him an allotment. We now meet for lunch, then go our own ways most of the day, meeting for dinner and spending the evenings together.** 99

66 **It took us several years into retirement before we achieved a working compromise on activities and time. One of the best things we did was to utilize our spare bedrooms as a 'study' so we have a space to retreat to and to keep our things in without being interrupted.** 99

Communication

Things to bear in mind if you're sharing your home with your partner:

- Proper communication between you and your partner is more important than ever; it's not so easy to walk away from an argument when you're at home together for longer.

- Be aware of how you and your partner are both feeling. Does one of you appear to be depressed by retirement? Is one of you trying to be "boss"? Have you divided up the household chores to everyone's satisfaction? Instead of bottling up concerns, talk to each other.

- If there are problems in your relationship, they will need to be addressed and fixed – otherwise they will get worse.

- You both need to be ready to listen, and to assert your own needs calmly and clearly.

- You should feel free to have your own space and do your own thing; if you feel your partner is being dismissive of your new interests, think about how to communicate why they are important to you.

- Discuss financial decisions that affect you both.

- If any of these things are difficult for one or both of you, Michael Longhurst's book *The Beginner's Guide to Retirement* walks you through tackling such tricky territory step by step, with exercises.

Quality Time

Perhaps you haven't always been there for all the people in your life, or at least not as much as you'd like. You may have had to miss family events in the past because of work commitments. Your partner understood why you couldn't always have dinner together. Your friends knew you were busy. But now that time is on your side, make sure those you care about are aware of it, and make up for lost time if you can.

Take the time to call, email or visit. Connect with people now, before it's too late and they've moved on. Invite them to do something with you – perhaps a walk in the botanic gardens, or a visit to an exhibition, or watching a film. Make sure you choose something you think they'd enjoy, and don't make them feel pressured if they have commitments. Let them know you're available.

Getting together with friends needn't mean an expensive night out. If your friends are also retired, they should understand that it's the meeting up that's important.

Loneliness

Older people are especially vulnerable to loneliness and social isolation. Cut off from their work or no longer the hub of the family, people can easily drift into social isolation. Whatever the cause, it's easy to feel alone and vulnerable, which can then lead to a decline in mental and physical health.

Many older people suffering loneliness find it hard to reach out and ask for help. But there are a number of ways to combat loneliness and connect with others, even if you live alone and find it hard to get out.

- **Seek out opportunities to connect with people. Get out, whether it's to a park, cafe, community centre or just the local shop. Smile and say hello.**

- **Invite a friend or neighbour over for a coffee.**

- **Contact your national or regional/local charity for older people. Many will organize social evenings and outings for older people in your area, and they will facilitate meetings to help you integrate.**

- **Ring a friend or relative.**

- **Learn to accept people's genuine offers of help with good grace – most people love to help, and that's not patronizing.**

- All the other suggestions in this book will also help: join clubs, get out and about, keep your diary full (but not too full!) of engaging activities, connect with friends and family through social media, volunteer and start some new interests. Having some engaging hobbies at home to help you enjoy your time alone – instead of seeing it as a big scary space needing to be filled – can be hugely rewarding.

Caring

Many people find themselves in a caring role as they grow older – often for an ailing relative or partner. If you find yourself in this situation, seek advice and assistance. Local authorities and charities are there to help. The job of caring can be mentally and physically exhausting, and in most countries you'll be entitled to financial, physical and psychological support. Don't feel guilt-tripped into never taking a break; accept and seek offers of respite care. You need to look after yourself first and foremost, and you will need a break. Even if the cared-for person isn't happy with this, a week or two of respite care can really help you to rest, recover, do something enjoyable for you, and return to your care commitments with renewed energy. Various support charities offer drop-in sessions or organize outings for cared-for people.

Nurturing Positive Friendships

Here are some tips on how to maintain healthy platonic relationships:

- Be a supportive friend. This doesn't mean going around doling out advice; it means offering support and genuine care. Learn to know when to give your opinion and when to hold back.

- Practise really listening. This is one of the greatest life skills we can learn and one of the greatest gifts we can give the people in our lives. If you find yourself wanting to jump into a conversation, practise discipline. Show respect to the speaker and give them your full attention.

- Don't be afraid to confide in your friends. Don't be the one who holds all their cards to their chest and never lets anyone in.

- Show your true self – don't hide behind a perfect facade. Nobody really likes the friend who always has to brag or prove they're just a little bit better than everyone else.

- The Joy of "No": Learn when to say no. You don't always have to say yes to everything.

- Friendships aren't about material things, but the occasional handwritten note or card or handmade gift can be a lovely personal way to remind your friend how much you value their friendship.

Good Grandparenting

It's widely acknowledged that the relationship between grandparents and grandchildren is a uniquely special one. Grandparents can indulge their grandkids, lavish them with attention, abstain from the trickier bits of parenting such as broken sleep, anxieties, social difficulties or fussy eating, and hand them back after a few hours to settle in front of their favourite show for the evening. Essentially, grandparents get to cherry-pick all the good stuff and not worry too much.

Grandparents have an enormous influence on grandchildren, and the bond can be one of mutual appreciation and unconditional love. If the parents work long hours, this is your opportunity to step in and develop a close bond with your grandchild. If you put in the time and effort, your relationship with them can be one of the most satisfying things in your life. It also adds a new dimension and level of respect with your own children, if you're heavily involved in their children's lives. If they live far away, get into using a video chat app so you can chat face to face when you can't be with them.

Things to Do with the Grandkids

- Read to them. Introduce them to books you think they'll love – and even better, take them to the library to introduce them to the joy of choosing their own books.

- Bake together.

- Take them to a show.

- Take them on a wildlife walk and point out all the different creatures, bugs, birds, trees and plants that you see. Don't hurry. Let them pick up feathers and cones, etc.

- Paint together. Let them get messy.

- Take them exploring in the woods, and build a den. You can download a tree and animal tracks identifier app or look for burrows and nests.

- Gather some items such as cones and leaves and make some wild art. Look up Pinterest for inspiration and ideas.

- Paste together a scrapbook.

- Build jigsaws and models together.

- Do a treasure hunt around the house or garden.

- Take them swimming.

- Take them on a trip to a safari park or zoo.

- Show them that doing a good turn for someone can be rewarding.

- Encourage them to create a play or a music routine to perform.

- Take them to a petting farm.

- Help them with a school project.

- Show them old photograph albums and tell them stories from your own childhood.

Don't Have Grandkids?

Plenty of retired people don't have grandchildren. Perhaps you don't even like kids? But if you do, and if you envy friends who're always going on about how many grandkids they have, is there anyone in your neighbourhood or circle of friends who would be happy for you to mind their kids sometimes? Several countries have foster or bonus grandparent schemes – you register to be a voluntary foster grandparent for a specific family. For some older people, this can be a wonderful way to reduce loneliness and enjoy a close relationship with one or more young people.

Tracing Your Family History

Investigating your family history is interesting and satisfying, as everyone is a little bit curious about past members of their clan and what kind of people they might have been. There are a number of websites that can help with your research (most of which you need to pay to get full access to) and you could even convert your findings into a written account of your own. If you don't particularly like writing, you could design a visual map or even make a video retelling your findings. There are no hard and fast rules about how you record the fruits of your research.

The obvious place to start is with your living relatives – the older the better. Hopefully they will appreciate your interest and enjoy the opportunity to talk about their memories. This interaction might even lead to friendships with long-lost connections or those with whom you'd only ever had passing contact. If the final story you piece together would be of interest to the rest of the family or to future generations, perhaps you'll want to make a few printed copies.

How to Do the Research

Seek out photograph albums, diaries and letters, from as many sources as possible.

Search online, both to access information and to utilize the available resources.

National libraries are full of useful information, as are census and immigration records.

Your subjects are real people who have led interesting lives. Military records, records of service in occupations such as the merchant navy, and even, in more lurid cases, prison records are waiting to be explored.

Scrapbooks, memorabilia collections, old school reports – it is all grist to your mill; use these to find common points of interest and develop an angle on the story you want to tell.

Look for the telling details, the elusive facts. You are, in a sense, a detective, uncovering meaning in a murky past.

Social networks like Facebook and Twitter will help you make useful and, at times, unexpected connections.

Joining a family history society might also prove useful.

Companionship

If you live alone and just haven't met a special someone for some time, don't let yourself get lonely. Make an effort to make new friends if old ones move away. Reach out to others and find activities that involve social contact, such as a book or bridge club. If the house feels too big, you might consider getting a lodger or even house-sharing with a trusted friend.

But if you're one of the many who would like to find something more romantic, then don't fall into the trap of thinking you've left it too late. Meeting people in a group is far easier than one on one, so get out there and follow your dream, and see where it leads. If your retirement plans involve travel, why not try a singles holiday?

City Life

City life can be better if you're single and retired. Why? There's so much to do that's easily available in a city, from museums, cinemas and theatre, art events and university courses – all free or discounted for seniors – to coffee shops and good-value eateries, and of course a wider variety of people with whom to interact.

Finding Love Online

The fastest-growing cohort using online dating sites is yours – midlife and beyond – and some sites are especially made for the fabulous over-fifties and super over-sixties. Ask around to see if any of your friends have enjoyed using a particular site. Try to find one where people's profiles seem honest. Sometimes fees to join a more exclusive site can pay off because they have better filters.

Finding a site that pitches itself as a "friendship and dating site" can make the chatting online more natural. By making it clear you're interested in social friends as well as dating, there's no pressure if you like someone but don't see them immediately as a potential mate. The upside of internet dating is that you never know who you might meet – they might have similar goals to you, they could have had a fascinating life, but you might never have met them otherwise.

Safety First

Find a site you trust and beware of scams. Don't put yourself in a dangerous situation by agreeing to meet a stranger somewhere that's not public, telling them where you live, or giving away too many personal details, however nice they seem.

Four-Legged Friends

A dog or cat can provide immeasurable comfort and companionship in retirement. They don't answer back, they smother you in unconditional love, and they are a warm body to cuddle up with in the evening.

In the case of dogs, they also get you out for daily walks, thereby helping with your fitness and social connectedness too. Yes, they're a bind, and you have to arrange for a friendly face to look after them if you go away, plus there are vet fees to think about and food to provide. However, dog-lovers around the world agree dogs give far more to your life than they take.

Cats are lower maintenance than dogs and they also provide wonderful company, especially for people who live alone, often warming your bed for you or curling up on your lap if you're relaxing. If you're considering a dog or cat as a pet, visit a rescue centre and take your time visualizing a particular furry companion in your life.

9

TRAVEL

Perhaps the biggest retirement dream is the freedom to travel. No longer confined to short holiday periods fitted in around your working life, now is your opportunity to do something more ambitious. You could take a longer trip – whether abroad or close to home – and you don't have to worry about returning to a giant pile of paperwork.

For many people, the dream is already firmly in place as they wave goodbye to their old colleagues: time to hop around the Maldives with no imminent flight home, or go volunteering in Sri Lanka for a few months. The key is to keep it relatively cheap – aided by the fact that you can now be flexible on travel dates and pick up discounts. Make the most of it by finding the right means of travel for you, and knowing what you want to get out of it.

**" TO SOME OF US,
RETIREMENT GIVES
US TIME TO FOLLOW
OUR DREAMS. "**

Shirley Mitchell

A Holiday from What?

If you're not working, why do you need a holiday? There are many reasons why getting away can increase your happiness level during retirement and give you fresh energy:

- A break from routine that may encourage you to break with habits.

- Making new friends.

- Learning new things about the world and yourself.

- Taking on new challenges and having unexpected new experiences.

- Fun and laughter away from your everyday environment.

- A new perspective on your life.

- Pushing your boundaries.

- No longer taking things for granted.

- Setting new goals and evaluating your life.

Airbnb

Airbnb.com is an online site that allows you to rent unique places to stay – usually a room, apartment or entire house, but there are also windmills, lighthouses, treehouses, yurts, boats, castles and private islands...

You rent direct from the owners and, at its most basic, it can be a way to stay affordably in an interesting place. Some set-ups allow you to meet your hosts, who are proud to show off their interesting home and their corner of the world. One great benefit of Airbnb is that you're staying in an actual neighbourhood rather than a hotel surrounded by other tourists. So you live like a local; there might be a local market nearby and neighbourhood restaurants. Often you have access to a whole home, meaning it's perfect for longer stays; you'll have a kitchen, and maybe a collection of books to read while there.

To offset your costs – though Airbnb properties are usually cheaper than hotels – you can list your own home on the same site. It's easy and it opens up a whole new world of adventures. If you're not sure where you want to go but love the idea of something different, search out where the best bargains are to be had. Browsing the site is bound to give you the travel bug!

Happy House-Sitting

Discover the world of house- and pet-sitting, where you can get to know a new place absolutely free – except for the fee of signing up to a website. All you have to do is look after someone's home, garden and pets while they're away. If you're feeling the need for a change of scenery, and you're a capable person who loves animals, the world is your oyster.

The most exciting part about house-sitting is that it offers a way to stay in a place you'd love to go. You could hunt for house-sits on a Mediterranean island or a beachside town in Mexico, find yourself a mountain retreat in France or an eco-cabin in the Adirondacks. As long as you demonstrate you're a responsible individual or couple with an aptitude for maintaining a property and looking after pets, these places can be yours to enjoy. It's travel without the cost of accommodation or eating out. Homeowners often specify that they're looking for a retired person, as they want a mature, capable person they can trust to spend time with their pet.

Sites include www.mindmyhouse.com and www.nomador.com.

Staycations

Since the Covid-19 pandemic, many people have discovered the joy of a vacation at home. You get all the benefits – sightseeing, day trips, meals out – without the cost of accommodation and travel costs. You get to see your local area from the perspective of a tourist, then return to the comfort of your own bed.

For inspiration on things to do and places to go, visit your tourist information centre in person or online. You could also look up TripAdvisor for top things to do in your city or region. This is another benefit of the staycation: you discover all sorts of interesting things, businesses and activities you've never taken the time to notice before, from quirky backstreet cafes to charming art studios. It can give you a renewed pride and joy in your locality, and you'll be able to recommend your favourite leisure activities, day trips, museums and sites to any friends or family visiting the area. You could even write about your staycation in your blog, or post images on social media.

Motorhome Magic

Be it an RV ("recreational vehicle"), housebus, Winnebago, or just a little caravan or campervan, a mobile abode is your ticket to being at home wherever you are on the road.

Embrace your inner hippie and take off with your guitar and a pile of books, or just a heap of curiosity and an open mind. With a motorhome you can stay in a campsite right on the edge of the wildest stretch of coast, and still have some of your creature comforts.

If you love travelling so much that you want to spend more of the year on the road, RV and caravanners' websites offer camaraderie, technical support, discussion forums, rallies and invaluable tips on everything from choosing the right RV for you to living better with less.

Details, Details

If you decide to stay on the road for more than a few weeks at a time, then you may want to make arrangements for your post to be forwarded. Get organized about paying your bills online and make sure your health insurance will cover you wherever you are.

You're Never Too Old to Camp

Camping is a hugely affordable way to travel and discover a country or area. The vast network of campsites around the world varies from tiny, boutique or remote to giant campsites with multiple restaurants, major leisure facilities and daily entertainment. Many larger sites have pre-pitched tents or static homes to choose from, and many offer dog-friendly options.

Whether it's coastal, cities or lakeside you fancy, and whether it's home or overseas, various websites offer a huge range of options to suit every budget.

Hostels and Backpackers

For some reason, older people often seem to forget about hostelling as an option. Many hostels now have bars and restaurants, log fires, games rooms, quiet rooms, a few private en-suite bedrooms, a never-ending supply of hot water and other facilities. The same ethos remains, however: hostelling is about sharing accommodation with like-minded people, opening your horizons and talking to people from all over the world. It remains an excellent option for affordable travel, and you're bound to meet someone interesting.

Sail Off into the Sunset

Sailing isn't the cheapest hobby but, like many dreams, it's affordable if you're prepared to make sacrifices elsewhere. If you own your home, it's possible you could downsize in order to rent or own a modest sailboat and see some beautiful places. You could offset some costs by renting out your home for the months you're away.

If you don't have a lot of money to invest but would love to fulfil the dream, those who have managed to do it recommend that you sign up for a course of lessons, read everything you can, and don't give up. Jan Irons met her husband David on a sailing course and, once retired, they spent six months a year in the sunny Caribbean, living cheaply like locals and eating fish they caught themselves. "My husband had one rule: Whatever we did when we retired, it had to be done in shorts."

> ## Do Something Completely Different for a Year
> Remember how quickly your birthday used to roll around when you were on the work treadmill? It didn't seem possible that 12 months had passed, yet within that time you could have had the adventure of your life. Now you can!

A Place in the Sun

For years you've had to live in a particular place because of your job. Now, you're free to choose. If you're not necessarily tied to the place you currently live, perhaps it's time to think about a change.

If you're hankering after something more exotic and if there are no visa restrictions stopping you, you may be able to reduce your living costs by moving to a country that's cheaper and warmer. Downsize or sell up if you need to in order to move to your dream life. A new life might even inspire you to start a new part-time business, or write about your experiences. There is much to be gained from the experience of a different culture.

Try Before You Buy

It's not always advisable to sell up unless you've done your research – you don't want to lose all your savings if things go wrong, after all. Renting a place can be a good way to find out whether your dream move is actually right for you. Something that was at first exciting and exotic can sometimes not live up to that reality once it has become your everyday life, especially if you miss friends, family and your home culture.

Ten Books to Inspire You

Getting away from it all isn't always possible, but if you have a spare room, conservatory or shed, how about converting it into a library so you can escape with your imagination? Here are some inspiring books to take with you...

Chickens, Mules and Two Old Fools – Victoria Twead's hilarious story of moving to a Spanish village with her partner Joe.

Eat, Walk, Write: An American Senior's Year of Adventure in Paris and Tuscany – Boyd Lemon retires from law aged 69 and moves to Europe for a fulfilling year.

Journeys of a Lifetime – *National Geographic*'s compilation of 500 of the world's greatest trips, complete with stunning photographs. From cruises around Antarctica to horse treks in the Andes, this ultimate bucket list of adventures is bound to leave you salivating for foreign shores.

In a Sunburned Country (titled *Down Under* in the UK) – Bill Bryson's hilarious journey through the baked deserts and colourful coastline of Australia, trying not to get attacked by deadly snakes and spiders.

The Geography of Bliss – Eric Weiner journeys from America to India in search of what makes a population happy. A blend of anecdotes, science and psychology, delivered with humour.

Narrow Dog to Carcassonne – Terry Darlington and his wife, on retirement, decided to sail a narrowboat across the Channel and down through France to the Mediterranean.

Greece on My Wheels – Edward Enfield, recently retired and fuelled by a love of all things Greek, cycles rugged paths contemplating Byron, Lear and classical history.

Dog Days in the Fortunate Islands: A New Life in Hidden Tenerife – John Searancke and his wife retire to the quiet north of Tenerife, learn Spanish and explore local cuisine.

The Olive Farm – Carol Drinkwater's adventures at a Provençal olive farm which she and her partner set about restoring.

Walking the Camino – Tony Kevin describes himself as an "overweight, sedentary, 63-year-old former diplomat" as he sets off with just a backpack on a gruelling eight-week trek to Santiago de Compostela.

Worldwide City Breaks

Author's Top 25 Interesting Cities to Visit:

Tokyo, Japan

Amsterdam, Netherlands

Beijing, China

Jaipur, India

Sydney, Australia

Hanoi, Vietnam

Dubrovnik, Croatia

Bangkok, Thailand

Rio de Janeiro, Brazil

Rome, Italy

Barcelona, Spain

New York, USA

Cape Town, South Africa

London, UK

Moscow, Russia

Dubai, United Arab Emirates

Singapore

Budapest, Hungary

Marrakesh, Morocco

Santiago, Chile

Cairo, Egypt

Kathmandu, Nepal

Seoul, Korea

Siem Reap, Cambodia

Paris, France

10

PURPOSE AND FULFILMENT

You've left behind one kind of stress – the deadlines, the commuting – but don't be surprised if another type starts to nag away at you. Retirement may come as a shock to the system: a culture shock. If you're the type of person who lived for their work 24/7, and you don't have friends that aren't colleagues or business associates, then you may experience an identity crisis if you don't have other interests and social circles to keep you satisfied.

Look at it positively – the greater the life change, the more rewarding it can be. An emotional upheaval might end up as an opportunity to get to know yourself better. You may find what you really want, whether it's spending more time with family and friends, or fulfilling your potential in any number of other areas. This is when you get to discover the new you.

Deep down, our sense of purpose comes from within. Dig around and unearth yours.

"**RETIRE THE WORD *RETIREMENT* FROM YOUR VOCABULARY... DOESN'T *RENAISSANCE* OR *GRADUATION* OR *TRANSITION* BETTER DESCRIBE YOUR POST-CAREER LIFE?**"

Marika Stone

Something Missing?

A sense of purpose is an essential human desire for living a meaningful life, yet it is something that evades many of us throughout our careers. How many of us in our 9–5 feel purpose is a slippery thing that we seek but cannot really realize? Some work for employers they don't respect; some don't feel any great value in their work; some are plagued by the feeling "but what's the *point*?" Others may have enjoyed a great deal of fulfilment in their jobs, and may feel they have made a useful contribution. Either way, retirement is an unparalleled opportunity to really seek out something rewarding and meaningful to do with the rest of your life.

Retirement can be a time to really question what matters to you, and what would give you a sense of joy, satisfaction and self-worth. Often, giving something back can be the answer – the benefits for both giver and recipient are boundless.

Defining Yourself

Many struggle to adjust to being no longer needed, once the initial euphoria of liberation from the "daily grind" has worn off. How can your old workplace function without you? Even if you're proud of the legacy you've left, it can leave you feeling your life lacks direction; without work, you can feel rudderless. So what are you going to do about it?

Finding a new way to define yourself – not by a job title – is going to be important. When you're introduced to someone and aren't sure what you do any more, find a light-hearted way to fill the space in the conversation until you figure it out. You could always try responding, "Whatever I like!"

You may also need something to belong to. Clubs, societies, classes and community organizations will all give you something to identify with. A volunteering commitment can also give you a routine and a place where you are needed and valued, if you find life in retirement too lacking in structure. If you require discipline to ensure you get outdoors and meet people, a part-time role could be just what you need to help you to enjoy your leisure time more.

Volunteering

" **If you want happiness for an hour, take a nap. If you want happiness for a day, go fishing. If you want happiness for a year, inherit a fortune. If you want happiness for a lifetime, help someone else.** "

Anonymous

Research shows performing acts of kindness makes people feel more energized, less angry and more cheerful. Doing something kind or helpful gives us the same neurological joy response as pleasure, according to the US National Institutes of Health. Meanwhile, a high degree of altruism within a society is vital in order for that society to consider itself happy and operate positively, according to the World Happiness Report. People who volunteer their time are not only happier; they enjoy a more meaningful life and suffer less anxiety and depression. Meik Wiking, CEO of the Happiness Research Institute in Copenhagen, explores this and much more in his uplifting book *The Little Book of Lykke*.

Volunteering in your community provides an invaluable service to those in need and simultaneously boosts your own well-being. Interaction with others and feeling useful give you social connection and purpose. Most towns will have a centre of some kind that matches up volunteers with causes. National and international volunteering sites can be helpful in finding specific roles or simply ideas about what might be out there.

Good Deeds to Consider:

- Hospitals – hospices and large hospitals are always in need of volunteers to help with patients and family support.

- Charity shop assistant.

- Visitor guide at an art gallery or museum, or perhaps at your favourite natural heritage site.

- Maintenance or gardening.

- Working with a mental health charity.

- Providing meals on wheels.

- Administrative, marketing or lobbying work for a cause you believe in.

- Animal rescue – feeding and exercising the animals.

- Working with children with special needs.

- Befriending the elderly, either in an official capacity or simply in your neighbourhood.

- Homeless shelter assistance.

- Blood donation (different countries have different age restrictions; in Australia you can continue to donate until the day before your 76th birthday).

- First aid training or other health outreach.

- Sports events, such as directing crowds and handing out water at marathons. Parkrun is one organization that relies on its army of weekly volunteers.

Men's Sheds

Men often find themselves isolated and alone when they retire from work. While women traditionally find it easier to get involved in charity work informally, or join groups such as the Women's Institute, there have been fewer group activities especially for men.

So instead of retreating to your own shed in the garden, consider the phenomenon called Men's Sheds. Originating in Australia, it soon spread to other countries, providing a tool share and meeting place where men can find projects to work on together, making the most of their technical skills and experience. At a Men's Shed in Antrim, Northern Ireland, for example, the men opened a charity shop to raise the funds to build, equip and staff two schools in a poverty-stricken area of Ethiopia.

The Shed is a place for ideas to brew, as well as a sense of belonging to something worthwhile. If there isn't one in your area, perhaps you should think about starting one with a few friends, or placing a local ad for others who might like to join.

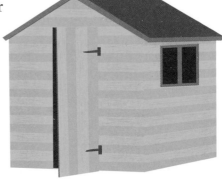

Personal Growth and Psychological Health

Professor Carol Ryff, Director of the Institute on Aging at the University of Wisconsin-Madison, has pinpointed six components of psychological health:

1. **Self-acceptance – accepting yourself as you are, with all your strengths and weaknesses.**

2. **Positive relatedness – caring for and identifying with others.**

3. **Autonomy – living your own life, rather than following the dictates of others.**

4. **Environmental mastery – creating surroundings that suit your personal needs and capacities.**

5. **Personal growth – continuing to develop your personal potential through learning and experience.**

6. **Purpose in life – continuing to be creative and productive.**

She noted that education increased the potential for personal growth and purpose in life. A sense of purpose is often achieved by charity work or active involvement in an organization aligned with our personal beliefs that can make a difference in the world.

General Tips for Finding Fulfilment

Think of people you admire or find inspiring. Can you emulate them somehow?

Have no regrets.

Forgive and move on. Try not to dwell on the past.

Appreciate the small things: whether it's natural sights or human touches, actively choose to observe the finer details in life.

Make a point of always showing your gratitude – "thank you" costs nothing.

Liberate yourself from self-limiting beliefs.

Respect your own time, and that of other people.

Be true to yourself.

Mentoring

Why waste all that knowledge and experience – why not pass it along to the younger generation through teaching, mentoring or coaching? It can give you a sense of achievement with every single session. Volunteer teachers are much in demand in developing countries, and practical skills can be particularly useful, especially in the health field. The VSO (Voluntary Service Overseas) organization is respected for its high-quality programmes.

If you've worked in business, then perhaps a start-up entrepreneur would value your mentorship. Imagine the satisfaction of seeing a business flourish thanks to your advice. Young entrepreneurs may have the ideas and energy, but the odds of turning their passion into something sustainable increase with the guidance of an experienced professional willing to look over their business plan, pass on knowledge and help solve problems.

Sports Coaching

If you're involved in a sports club but don't feel up to playing every week any more, you may find coaching the most useful role you've ever played. You'll still be part of the club, but without the injuries. Many clubs simply would not be able to function without volunteers and coaches, and many sports clubs welcome volunteers and support them through training programmes.

Plan Your Year

If you're used to working towards goals, then be your own boss, and set targets for yourself for the year. Give yourself an appraisal at the end of the year: have you achieved what you set out to do? Perhaps you'll be ready to take on more responsibility next year – or maybe you'll want to reduce your hours. Think about whether you're happy in your new life role.

Raising Funds for Charity

By the age of retirement, most of us have a cause of choice we'd like to do more about – the planet itself and its endangered species, poverty in a particular country, something closer to home in your community, or research for a disease. So do something about it in a bigger way by raising awareness and money. Here are some ideas of ways to raise money and make an impact:

- Open day of gardens in your area
- Sponsored something-a-thon
- Donate a percentage of sales of your book/ paintings/tickets for a show
- Fundraising bad poetry night
- Sell your garden produce and jams
- Sponsored 161-km (100-mile) bike ride
- Organize a live music and dance night and sell tickets
- Fundraising sports tournament
- Get your friends to create decadent cakes for an auction night

11

A LITTLE EXTRA

So what else is left? You've gone through all the joys of retirement but you still feel you should do something just a little bit silly before it's too late? You've been harbouring a closet desire to do something a little more left-field for decades?

Many of us have developed deep-rooted inhibitions since our carefree childhood years. It's time to dig up those roots, examine them, chop them up and throw them away. If there are things you've always secretly wanted to do or assumed you'd find the time or confidence to try at some point in your life, what's holding you back now? It's time for some proverbial grabbing of horns. Be outrageous. Do something daring. Step out of that jacket of conformity and be free!

If you take up any of the following, at least you'll never be stuck for dinner party conversation…

"BE ECCENTRIC NOW. DON'T WAIT FOR OLD AGE TO WEAR PURPLE."

Regina Brett

Pursue Your Childhood Dream

When she was young, growing up in Los Angeles, Andrea Peterson was rescued from a burning building by firefighters, and on being saved she told them she wanted to be one of them when she grew up. They laughed, saying she could be a good mother, maybe even a teacher or a nurse, but never a fireman. After a strict upbringing, she left behind her childhood dream and had various other jobs, including medical transcriptionist and professional ballerina – until she was 61, living in Vermont, when she read a newspaper article about riding in the town's ambulance to observe what they do. It sparked something inside her.

A neighbour who worked in the fire department allowed her to accompany him on duty one day, and they had an ambulance call; she found the situation rewarding and fulfilling, and started taking courses, wishing she'd done it earlier. At first the young guys on the firefighting course couldn't accept her. But at 66, Andrea Peterson received her certification and became a firefighter. "I had to wait a lifetime to be the real me," she wrote.

From the Sublime to the Ridiculous

Photograph as many species
of wildlife as possible.

Brew your own beer.

Start a nostalgia film club.

Get to grips with philosophy.

Get a job in a coffee shop to
gather material for
your novel.

Climb a very high mountain
(and stay there overnight).

Go into politics (not the best
way to make friends, though).

Learn to play a concerto.

Translate a book.

MEDIUM SUBLIME

VERY SUBLIME

Become a cheesemaker.

Open a jazz club.

Become a film extra (especially good as most parts are nonspeaking, so you don't have to memorize lines).

Go on a bike ride with your friend or partner on a bicycle made for two.

Start a novelty doily collection.

Swim with sharks.

MEDIUM RIDICULOUS

VERY RIDICULOUS

Video a dance routine with a group of friends and upload it onto YouTube.

Get a tattoo.

Take up rock climbing.

Learn sword juggling and fire breathing, and then set up a solo street show.

Invent Something

Peter Mark Roget was kept busy all his working life with his career as a medical doctor, but in his spare time during his early working years, he started classifying and cataloguing words according to their meaning. He had to put it aside eventually because of the demands of work, but after retiring at the age of 61, he spent the next few years working on his project. Known simply as "the thesaurus", it was finally published in 1852 – and after being revised many times, is still in print today. Aged 73 at the time of the first publication, Roget achieved quite a legacy in his retirement.

While Roget reportedly developed his list-making obsession as a coping mechanism to deal with depression, you don't need any physical or mental stimulus other than initiative to invent something in older age. If something has always fascinated you but you've never had time to properly investigate it, now's your opportunity.

Arabesque, Anyone?

John Lowe, a grandfather and former World War Two prisoner of war, started taking ballet lessons at the age of 79 and performed with a dance company into his nineties. "Dancing is the most amazing feeling," he said. "It is a joy to move to beautiful music." A former art teacher and theatre manager, he built himself a trapeze at home, laid a wooden floor and installed a ballet bar.

Lowe said he was making up for six years lost to World War Two, during which time he endured starvation in Japanese prison camps. The experience, he said, taught him that, "if I was determined enough, perhaps I could do anything."

Lowe, a pianist, had his first starring role at the age of 88, performing with dancers a quarter of his age. For him, the most energizing aspect was working with young people who treated him as a friend and equal rather than as an old man. Spending time with his children and grandchildren also kept him young at heart.

The takeaway message? Spend time with young people and continue to do things that give you a sense of youthful freedom and uninhibited joy.

Wacky Races*

Each year, thousands of people participate in extreme marathons, bicycle rides, triathlons and other endurance tests. They pit themselves against the elements in the most remote locations and take on the world's toughest challenges. This could be you.

Seriously, you're reading on? OK...

Of Scotland's 282 Munros – mountains higher than 914 m (3,000 ft) – Sgurr Dearg on the Isle of Skye is known as the Inaccessible Pinnacle, requiring a 50-m (164-ft) vertical rock climb.

Every June, triathletes meet to undertake the Escape from Alcatraz – a gruelling swim-cycle-run event from the infamous maximum-security prison to San Francisco.

From Eagle Plains, Yukon Territory to Tukyoyaktuk, Northwest Territories on the banks of the Arctic Ocean, the 6633 Ultra race is an extreme ultramarathon over 563 km (350 miles) with all your kit personally carried or pulled by sled. There is a shorter version of "only" 193 km (120 miles) if you're not that fit.

The Everest Marathon starts near Base Camp and follows 42.2 km (26.2 miles) over rough but spectacular mountain trails in the world's highest marathon every two years.

The Jungle Marathon is held in Brazil each October: choose between 101 km (63 miles) or 241 km (150 miles) of ultimate eco-race with 40-degree temperatures, swamps and river crossings, dense jungle canopy, 99 per cent humidity and the possibility of meeting a caiman, piranha or anaconda.

The Legendary Ultimate Challenge MudRun in Columbia, South Carolina, was designed and built by a former Marine drill instructor. Facing military-style obstacles day and night, they say "you will sweat, you will probably bleed, and yes, you might break some bones".

What – you're thinking of collecting tea cosies instead?

*We're not actually *recommending* you do any of these, unless you're a retired super-athlete aged 25.

Go for It, Grandpa and Grandma...

" I hope the record inspires others to realize it's never too late. "

Johanna Quaas, on being included in the Guinness World Records as the world's oldest gymnast

Feel a little bit past it? Simon Gandolfi, author of *Old Man on a Bike* and *Old Men Can't Wait*, spent his 70s travelling alone by motorcycle around India and the Americas. In 2019 Diane Hoffman, 91, broke the 400-m (1,312-ft) sprint world record in the 90–94 age group, having only run her first competitive track event at the age of 90 (she considered herself a tennis player, not a runner). In 2015, Charles Eugster, 95, author of *Age Is Just a Number*, set a 200-m (656-ft) world record for his age group, having only taken up sprinting at the age of 95. The former dentist and rower had also taken up bodybuilding at 87 because, he told his personal trainer, he was getting flabby and wanted a "beach-ready body". Helmut Wirz, a former pharmacist, became the world's oldest bungee jumper at the age of 87. And in 2013 Johanna Quaas, a retired PE teacher, was recorded as the world's oldest gymnast at 86. Some call it "ageing with attitude".

When American Lew Hollander completed an Ironman triathlon in October 2012 at the age of 82, he held the record as the world's oldest Ironman champion. An Ironman comprises a 4-km (2.4-mile) swim, a 180-km (112-mile) bike ride and a marathon run, without a break. His arch-rival is Sister Madonna Buder, aka the Iron Nun, who holds the record as the oldest woman ever to complete an Ironman triathlon, also at the age of 82. The Roman Catholic nun was inducted into the USA Triathlon Hall of Fame in Chicago aged 84. "If you don't think age and you just get up and do and you think you're a teenager, well, you'll start to act like one," she said.

Lew's Secret

To stay fit well into retirement, Ironman Lew Hollander recommends a healthy diet of nutrients and avoiding all processed foods. He also extols the benefits of a good, stable relationship and staying physically and mentally active.

Start a World-Famous Franchise

"Colonel" Harland Sanders, born in Indiana in 1890, started cooking for his family from the age of six after his father died and his mother had to go out to work. After doing a series of other jobs, at the age of 40 he was running a service station in Kentucky when he began cooking for hungry travellers, and eventually set up a restaurant across the street.

He was 65 when a new highway directed traffic away from his business, so he set about developing a franchise for his chicken recipe. Less than a decade later, there were 600 outlets of Kentucky Fried Chicken and he sold his interest in the company for $2 million. He went on to live to the grand old age of 90.

A Few Final Words of Wisdom

There is no old age. There is, as there always was, just you.
Carol Grace

It's not how old you are, it's how you are old.
Jules Renard

Old age is not a disease – it is strength and survivorship, triumph over all kinds of vicissitudes and disappointments, trials and illnesses.
Maggie Kuhn

Age is whatever you think it is. You are as old as you think you are.
Muhammad Ali

You can't help getting older, but you don't have to get old.
George Burns

You just don't let that rocking chair take over. You get up and go even if you don't want to.
Connie Reeves, centenarian cowgirl

CONCLUSION

What, then, is retirement? An end, or a beginning?

Luckily, retirement is not one-size-fits-all. Like children's moulding clay, it's perpetually pliable, and can be moulded and remoulded. Of course, the person who gets final say over the shape is you. Other people in your life and other commitments will be part of it – not all of us have the means or freedom to swan off to the Bahamas whenever we feel like it – but ultimately how you choose to spend your retirement, and what balance of physical, social and altruistic activities you decide works for you, is your call. And of course, that will evolve, as health and other commitments change.

The central maxim throughout this book, though, is to seize the opportunities in front of you. *Carpe diem, taking the bull by the horns...* Whatever cliché or proverb chimes with you, take inspiration from the souls featured within these pages, who have refused to accept that retirement is the end of the road.

So cast off those inhibitions if you can, and embrace your inner adventurer. Even if you're on a tight budget, there is so much out there for you to see and do. Above all, why not make every day count?

" RETIREMENT MAY BE AN ENDING, A CLOSING, BUT IT IS ALSO A NEW BEGINNING. "

Catherine Pulsifer

Have you enjoyed this book?
If so, why not write a review on your favourite website?

If you're interested in finding out more about our
books, find us on Facebook at **Summersdale Publishers**
and follow us on Twitter at **@Summersdale**.

Thanks very much for buying this Summersdale book.

www.summersdale.com